Grant Writing Made Easy

by

Maurene Hinds

Frank Schaffer Publications®

Author: Maurene Hinds

Editor: Sara Bierling

Interior Designer: Teather Uhrik

Frank Schaffer Publications®

Send all inquiries to:
Frank Schaffer Publications
8720 Orion Place
Columbus, Ohio 43240

Grant Writing Made Easy

ISBN: 0-7682-3078-0

4 5 6 7 8 GLO 12 11 10 09

Table of Contents

Introduction

What exactly is a grant? In order to qualify, most nonprofit organizations need to apply for 501(c)(3) nonprofit status with the federal government. Public schools fall into a special nonprofit status even though they are different than other nonprofit organizations. When a grantor gives you money, you are entering into a contract with that funder to perform activities as you have set out in your grant proposal.

Why a grant? The funds from grants can allow you to offer your students and faculty programs and training that might not be made available any other way. An effective grant funded project can give you the tools to create meaningful change in the lives of your students that the school or community could not otherwise accomplish. This can be both an exciting and overwhelming prospect.

Grant writing can be an intimidating process. Some funders require you to read through pages and pages of detailed instructions (and yes, you need to read every page). Federal grant applications tend to fall into this category. Other funders provide a paragraph or two of very general information. Individual donors often do not have any formal processes at all, requiring you to contact them through a query letter process. Some funders give you the option of submitting 30 pages of information; others want you to summarize your program in five pages or fewer. A federal grant application can be as many as 40 pages!

Where does this leave you? The good news is that all grants have some basic elements in common. Once you understand the fundamentals that all grants share, the process becomes much easier. You will complete a similar process for all grants that you write, tailoring each proposal to a specific funder.

For example, some funders only support medical research, while others only support educational programs. Obviously, you need to target appropriate funders. The second part of this is that some funders require a more formal tone than others. Does this mean you need to alter your program according to each funder? No. Your program will remain true to the needs you are trying to address. What it does mean is that you need to conduct careful research and emphasize the elements of your program that will appeal to your chosen funder. Show how your project meets the needs of the funder and the programs they prefer to support.

But before we get too far into the process, let us review a few "musts" to keep in mind before beginning.

1. While many people would probably not argue that many schools and special needs programs are grossly under funded, grants are not the solution to this problem. Grants must be developed to address a specific issue. This could include any number of programs or teacher training, but there must be a proven need for the grant aside from simply arguing that the school is under-funded in general. (Operational grants, which cover day-to-day operations, do exist, but most funders do not support this type of grant.)

2. Once you have developed your idea, you must write your grant to the specifications and instructions of your chosen funders. Failure to follow directions or to keep your funders' needs in mind can immediately put you out of the running. Funders publish guidelines on what types of grants they support and how to apply for those. All guidelines and directions must be carefully reviewed and followed if you want to have a chance at obtaining funding.

3. Write to your audience. This is a two-part issue. First, your chosen funder(s) have their own agendas that they use when deciding what grant requests to fund. For example, some funders only support medical research, while others only support educational programs. Obviously, you need to target appropriate funders. The second part of this is that some funders require a more formal tone than others. Does this mean you need to alter your program according to each funder? No. Your program will remain true to the needs you are trying to address. What it does mean is that you need to conduct careful research and emphasize the elements of your program that will appeal to your chosen funder. Show how your project meets the needs of the funder and the programs they prefer to support.

4. Do the research before writing your grant. The fact is that writing the actual grant is in many ways only a small part of the process. Extensive research is required throughout the process. There are many elements to a grant, as you will see in this book. Learn about all the required elements of a grant before you begin to try to write a proposal. You will need to conduct needs assessments, create a budget, and have a plan for how you will employ what you have learned through your program. These are not things that can be thrown together a few weeks or days before the submission deadline. Only after the proper research with supporting documents has been compiled can you successfully write a strong proposal.

5. Remember that the fruits of your labor have the potential to bring positive, lasting change to the lives of those students your programs and grant requests will help! Grant writing is a lot of work and takes a lot of time. But once you feel the thrill of writing a successful program, you will be able to see your efforts materialize for the benefit of your students.

The author would like to recognize the extensive grant writing training opportunity provided by Barbara C. Bader, Ph.D., and Steven Carr of Community Systems, P.O. Box 516, Bozeman, MT 59771-0516, 406-587-8970.

Chapter One: Planning

You know that your school, students, or community needs help. Perhaps your community consists of a high level of low-income families, or you have a large proportion of non-native English speaking students. How do you determine what needs to be done to help your community? Establishing a need for change in your school may be easy. The difficult part is determining how that need can best be addressed and then articulating possible solutions.

What if there are many needs, as is often the case? Developing a system for prioritizing needs will help determine where to start. Beginning with a smaller grant and working towards larger ones can also help shape the order in which you address the needs in your school and community. How you prioritize needs also depends on the tools you have available to conduct a project.

At a glance, what resources are available? How many people are able to commit to managing a grant? What size of a grant is realistic? There is no question that teachers are busy. But designing a program and creating a thorough proposal takes time and effort. Of course, there is the adage that if you want to get something done give it to a busy teacher! You do not want to completely overload your resources, though. People who are overextended will not be as effective in running the grant. Try to promote a "grant friendly" atmosphere in the school where staff and interested parties can be encouraged to participate and take time to work on the grant process. You may wish to hire substitutes for a day to allow teachers to work on grant proposals. The payoff could well outweigh the cost of the substitutes.

Mini-Grants

When resources are tight, consider beginning with a "mini-grant" (one under $5,000) rather than working on a large project that your school will not be able to support in the way of committed personnel. Many of these smaller grants can be found online and will only accept electronic submissions. Beginning with a smaller grant can also serve as inspiration to work towards larger grants. If there is a problem with getting people on board and supporting the grant process, the smaller grant can be used to demonstrate that the grant effort is worthwhile and can create positive results. Because there is no guarantee of obtaining funding, some people may be hesitant to put in the time and effort required to write a winning grant. Mini-grants, while still requiring time and dedication, are by their nature smaller and less intensive. Use them to gain support in the grant process. The additional benefit is that every grant adds to your reputation as a responsible grant manager, and you can use these when applying for larger grants. Having a history of successfully managing a previous grant, even a small one, can improve your chances of obtaining funding. Use this to your advantage and to gain support within your school and community if necessary.

Of course, if members of your team have experience in grant management, there is no reason to hold yourself back! Or, if you feel strongly that your students require a larger program in order to successfully meet the need it may be necessary to approach a funder for a larger grant. As long as you have the resources, go for it. The ultimate goal is to help as many students as possible.

When and How to Work

Work on your grant projects during "down" times: slower times of the day, month, or year. It is much easier to develop your grant program when you are not harried. The beginning of the school year, for example, is probably not the ideal time to be working on a grant proposal. Use the less hectic times to gather and organize grant material and work on the current grant application. If you find yourself up against a tight deadline, it might be worthwhile to wait another year rather than trying to hectically pull together a proposal. This may seem like a long time to wait, particularly when there is a real need for funds. But a proposal thrown together is much more likely to contain errors and reflect poorly on your school; something the reviewers might remember when you resubmit the following year after taking the necessary time. Working on tight deadlines also lends itself to less than ideal research and backup material or runs the risk of your not being able to obtain all the material you need. Why not wait it out and make the best impression you possibly can? Keep everything on file and work when you have time to think things through carefully.

If you are applying for a federal grant, you definitely want to give yourself plenty of time. Government applications can run up to 40 pages long and have very specific guidelines; obviously this is not something you want to tackle in a short amount of time. Government proposals are also very detail oriented, consisting of complex directions that must be followed exactly or your proposal will be thrown out. It will literally take hours—hours—to complete a thorough, well-written proposal. And by hours I mean days. Some studies have shown that a quality proposal can take up to 150 hours or more to complete. Do not let this scare you away, though. Government funding is a great option for educational projects and those requiring large amounts of funding. If your need requires extensive funding, a government grant can be the answer to your dreams. Winning a government grant is worth the time, effort, and personal satisfaction.

One of the first things you will want to do when beginning the grant process is develop a grant committee for your school or district. Grants, by their very nature, involve more than one person, not only in the development of a proposal, but also in the carrying-out of the plan once it has been funded. Grantors frequently like to see community involvement as well, particularly for government-funded programs or plans. Reach out to as many partners as possible right from the beginning. Not everyone will be involved all the time, but fostering those relationships early will make it easier to get the right people involved when you need it later on.

The benefits of creating a grant committee are many. When confronting a problem in your school and community, the more people involved, the more ideas can flow on how to solve those problems. While you do not want your grant committee to be too large, public input can be very helpful. Even when working with a smaller committee, public meetings can be used to gather more input on the needs in the school and community. Once you have determined how to address the need, different people on the committee can work on the various elements of the grant. While one person will be the grant writer, others can help conduct the needs assessment, do research, compose a budget, develop a timeline, and work on all the other issues that are involved in the grant-seeking process. You may find the help of your school or school system's reading coordinator, math coach, ESL coordinator, or Title I coordinator especially helpful.

Many projects require the knowledge of many people. Your grant committee members can each contribute to the project by providing skills in their area of expertise. An added benefit of this is that when people feel they are making a valuable contribution there is a higher level of commitment and ownership. Aim for a mixed group of people and skills when creating your team. This may require a bit of interviewing, determining others' interests, skills, and available time. Employing a broad range of individuals will also aid in the brainstorming processes that take place when generating and prioritizing proposal ideas.

Finally, the grant process requires support from a variety of sources, including fellow teachers, supervisors in the school system, parents, and other community members. By drawing from these various community members to serve on the grant committee, you can begin to obtain the support and commitment needed to see a grant proposal go from idea to written grant to obtaining funding to seeing the idea through to completion.

Grants require careful planning. Funds are typically awarded on a yearly basis. This means you have to plan ahead for the upcoming school year. And while some grants are available for multiple years, most are for a one-year timeframe. This means you have to develop plans for sustaining the project (keeping it going after the grant ends), or if you are developing a longer-term program, conduct careful planning to convince funders why they should support you for more than one year.

Once a grant committee is established, begin by developing some long-range grant plans. Prioritize short-term goals and only support grant efforts that lead to the immediate goals. Following success with the initial goals, the grant process will continue by looking to maintain the current success and building upon it with larger projects or by addressing the longer-term goals. Efficient grant writing is not writing a grant here and there. It involves developing and sustaining ongoing projects that can change people's lives.

Encourage any and all ideas to begin with; the group will prioritize as necessary. Because you will have a mix of people on your committee, including teachers, parents, and community members, you will have a broad range of suggestions. Ideas tend to spark more ideas. Take the ball and run for a while.

Project Evaluation Checklist

Name of Project _____

Project Timeline _____

Project Manager _____

❑ My project meets a strategic need in my school community.

❑ My project is supported by national or state standards.

Standards

❑ NCTE/IRA   ❑ NCTM   ❑ NSTA

❑ Head Start   ❑ NAEYC   ❑ NCSS

❑ Other _____   ❑ State Standards _____

❑ My project will involve students in the following grades and locations.

_____

❑ There is staff available to me who will support my project.

❑ My principal or administrator supports my project.

❑ I will evaluate the success of my project through the following methods.

❑ This project requires funding that CAN/CANNOT be found through community fundraising.

_____

❑ There are at least three public or private funding sources that can meet the budgetary needs of this project.

_____ _____ _____

Prioritizing Projects

Possible Project	The Need	Target Audience	Length of Project	Estimated Budget

 0-7682-3078-0 *Grant Writing Made Easy*

Long-Term Plans

Immediate Projects	One-Year Plan	Three-Year Plan

Published by Frank Schaffer Publications. Copyright protected.   0-7682-3078-0 *Grant Writing Made Easy*

Before You Begin

Create a checklist of everything you will need to keep track of during your grant writing process, such as:

- ✧ your primary target audience
- ✧ project ideas
- ✧ lists of all stakeholders
- ✧ lists of personnel
- ✧ letters of support
- ✧ publicity about your school
- ✧ potential and top-rated funders
- ✧ back-up documents

For the Proposal (to use during the process and again afterwards before you submit the final proposal):

- ✧ cover letter
- ✧ the title
- ✧ the abstract
- ✧ statement of need and supporting documents
- ✧ goals and objectives
- ✧ project methods (activities)
- ✧ work plans and timetables
- ✧ evaluation plan
- ✧ dissemination and utilization plans
- ✧ budget and supporting documents

Also create lists of people you need to be in contact with throughout the process and those from whom you will need to obtain signatures (such as the principal and board members). Keep track of everyone on the grant committee, what their specialty area is for the process, and how to contact them. Make this list available to everyone on the committee and schedule meetings at appropriate intervals.

What Types of Grant Projects?

Your desire to obtain grant funds for your students is likely twofold: first, you recognize a need and desire to help your students in need; and second, you understand the importance of maintaining a high level of instruction and services that will keep your school up-to-date with the Education Act (No Child Left Behind, or NCLB) requirements. The following list provides some areas that may spark ideas for you or help you articulate the problems you may be seeing in your school and community. Students in need may benefit from grants addressing:

- ✧ academic improvement for disadvantaged students
- ✧ students with limited English proficiency
- ✧ high teacher turnover
- ✧ high-poverty areas
- ✧ neglected or delinquent children
- ✧ children with disabilities
- ✧ refugee or immigrant children
- ✧ children facing discrimination
- ✧ reading/vocabulary programs
- ✧ special after school or tutoring programs
- ✧ teacher recruiting and training
- ✧ parental and community involvement
- ✧ school safety
- ✧ homework centers
- ✧ sex education
- ✧ literacy programs
- ✧ English as second language and immigrant issues
- ✧ parenting issues (both parents of students and teens as parents)
- ✧ phonics reading programs
- ✧ reduction of class size
- ✧ special education

Some specific ideas for grant projects are:

- ✧ staff development on use of manipulatives in reading or math
- ✧ utilizing brain research to improve the classroom environment
- ✧ after school tutoring by college education majors
- ✧ creating a book or resource room
- ✧ establishing a math night during which students and parents play games to learn math concepts
- ✧ after school program that focuses on math or science in the community setting
- ✧ after school program for art and music
- ✧ establishing a reading volunteer program

Once you have determined which area(s) is of most importance to your students, you will need to follow a few steps before researching available grants and writing the proposal. How can you know what types of funders to target if you do not have a clear understanding of what you are asking for? At this point, you know there is a need for improvement. A detailed needs assessment (documentation supporting the need for change) will be required for your grant (this will be covered in Chapter Three). Begin thinking about obtaining letters of support for the idea and determine what types of proof you will need to support your claim that this is indeed a need that is being neglected.

At this point, to help you focus your idea, you will want to develop some basic goals and objectives (these will also be covered in greater detail in Chapter Three). Because the terms "goals" and "objectives" are used frequently in grant writing, now is a good time to define the terms.

Goals describe the long-term, overall impacts of the project.

Objectives are the strategies that will be used to meet the goals. Objectives must be measurable, such as an increase in participation or improved test scores (the outcomes).

How do you develop goals and objectives? One of the best methods is to turn to your state's educational standards and incorporate national and NCLB guidelines. Reviewing these materials will help focus the project. Consider using some of the same language when writing your goals and objectives as is used in the state guidelines and in the NCLB act, particularly when writing applications for federal grants.

For example, California's state guidelines for grade six Written and Oral Language Communications include the following: "Students write and speak with a command of Standard English conventions appropriate to this grade level." Students who are learning English as a second language will obviously have difficulties meeting this requirement. An after-school communications program could have "improve language capabilities for sixth-grade students" as a goal with an objective of "students will demonstrate improved vocabulary skills measured by consistent testing at regularly-scheduled intervals throughout the program."

Defining Your Audience

Funders will require specific information on who will be served and why, how many will be served, and what the expected outcomes will be. Why should a funder support your program over another applicant's? Many schools want to "improve reading skills" or "reduce drop-out rates" or "prevent teen pregnancy." These broad descriptions will not suffice when seeking grant support. Funders are, out of necessity, becoming more and more stringent in their requirements. As a grant writer, it is up to you to clearly state who will benefit from your request and what the specific outcomes will be. Who will improve reading scores and by how much? Whose drop-out rates will be reduced and by how much? Will both boys and girls be targeted in a teen pregnancy program, and will it be all students or a specific segment of your student population? Your outcomes must be scientifically measurable.

Say, for example, you want to create a program that will assist non-native English speakers. Not only will you want to inform your funder of the

numbers of English language learners that will be
served, you will want to go even further. You should
outline the number of students, their origins, family
history, and poverty issues, and compare those statistics
to national ones.

Your grant proposal needs to not only define who is in
need of intervention and why, but to also show that the
target group is not receiving help anywhere else, or that
additional help is needed if they are. In order to accomplish
this, you need to carefully assess your idea before proceeding
further, and conduct preliminary research to verify your beliefs.

Assessing Your Idea

Potential funders have a lot of questions that will need to be answered before
they will even consider your request. A successful grant proposal can only be
created if you are able to provide strong, supported answers. Asking yourself and your
committee a few key questions before getting too deep into your project will save a lot of
time and effort by highlighting the projects strengths and weaknesses. It will also help you
fine-tune the idea, which will make the grant writing process that much easier and will
guide your continuing research efforts.

Funders will want to know, and you will need to address in your proposal, the following
items:

- an overview of the project; can you sum up the key components in a few
  sentences?
- why the project is needed; what is the purpose of the project?
- what the activities will be to meet the project goals
- who will be involved, and what will each person do
- which at-risk students will benefit from your project
- how will you evaluate the project; what key indicators will exist to show whether or
  not the project was successful?

After the target population has been identified and defined, the next issue to address is a
need for the idea. Conducting a needs assessment will help you determine if the need
actually exists, how many people are affected, and to what extent (more information on
needs assessments can be found in Chapter Three). Another important aspect of
determining the need is to also establish the consequences of not addressing the issue.

As obvious as it may sound, you also need to determine if the idea is a good one. Have
similar programs been tried and failed? Are you looking to continue doing what you have
been doing (an operational grant), and if so, is what you are doing working? Funders are
not likely to support an operational grant if the current activities are not producing results.
Do you have the time and resources to carry-out the project? Is everyone involved
committed to the project? (This is very important. The excitement of winning a grant quickly
fizzles if the people involved are not dedicated to seeing it through.) Is the project of a
reasonable size and scope that you will be able to see the idea through to completion?

Many funders like to know if the idea is a new one, or if it is a program that is being adopted from another source. If it is an adopted program, how has the program benefited students in other areas? What types of changes will you make, if any, for your particular situation? If it is a new idea, how will the grant benefit students beyond your immediate area? Public funders in particular like to see how a program or idea can be of benefit to others. Will you be able to share your success with other teachers, schools, and students? How do you plan to share the information? Creating a project that can have local, state, and national benefits can be very appealing to some grantors. Demonstrate how your project can easily be adapted for other schools. Show your dedication to creating a model that other teachers can easily use to incorporate your program into their teaching activities or to recreate the program at their school.

Tools and Resources

What tools and resources do you need in order to reach your goals and objectives? Chances are good you need additional tools in order to make change happen; if you had the tools you needed, you might not need to apply for a grant. The required tools can take many forms. Examples of tools include books, proven programs, technology needs, etc. The tools you need must be shown to be required for your grant. This is not the place to try to squeeze in some extra materials that you cannot afford to purchase otherwise. Grantors are wary of and look for tools that are not necessary. Resources include personnel needed to carry-out the program. Personnel needs are often a mix of existing staff and new or temporary hires. Bringing in experts is often a great way to ensure the program is a success.

Also keep in mind that many grantors do not fund "bricks and mortar" needs. While construction grants do exist, the tools we are talking about here are the equipment and resources that you will need to make your program a success.

For both your program and your staffing needs, think new, new, and new. Grantors do not want to fund you to do the "same old" programs that are in place now unless you are seeing phenomenal success but do not have the funds to continue. Grants are not a means for providing raises to your staff. To meet the personnel needs and make your program a reality, chances are good you will need to bring in outside help. Think of this as a great opportunity to bring in someone who can lead or direct the program in a way that will bring great benefits to your students and provide training to your current staff.

Other than additional personnel, who else will be involved in your grant project? Many funders, particularly public grantors, like to see community involvement. Look for ways to partner with other groups in your community (and of course, seek cooperation and approval before writing a formal grant proposal with the partner mentioned as a participant). Say, for example, you have a large population of Spanish-speaking students but only one teacher on staff who speaks Spanish. You know that your community has a YMCA with multiple staff members who speak Spanish. How can you develop a proposal that can incorporate the skills in your community with your school's needs?

How can you create a relationship with the YMCA that will be mutually beneficial? Do not limit yourself when generating partnership ideas.

Do not limit the number of organizations and individuals you can partner with. School is only one aspect in a child's life—an important one, yes, but students, particularly those in the high-poverty and high crime-rate areas, need all the support they can get. Use your community to create positive working relationships and collaborate on projects to help your students. Communicate with potential partners throughout the year and throughout the process. You will likely be seeking additional grants following the initial project. If you cannot use a potential partner in the immediate future, it may be the perfect relationship for the grant project that is next on the list. Cultivate and draw on those important relationships.

Are Those Tools and Resources Available?

Having a great idea is one thing; being able to complete the project is another. Coming up with a great solution to a problem will not help anyone unless the appropriate resources are available or can be made available.

Make sure that you can actually bring in outside help if you need it, and that the school staff you are counting on will have the time to help. Also make sure you are not assuming you will have parental help or be able to use school facilities. Do your homework and make sure you have guaranteed promises from people who understand fully the commitment you are asking for.

Is It Appropriate and Cost Effective?

Your students may be at risk for failure or low grades due to poverty and poor nutrition. Is a school program on nutrition the best way to address this problem? Or would it be more appropriate if another organization got involved to help families in need find gainful employment? Or is the ideal situation one in which you collaborate with a community organization to provide both nutritional education in school and employment support outside school for the families? Only you can determine if your idea is appropriate for the school setting; however, knowing that there is a need and addressing it in the best possible way may not be a school-related issue.

Another equally-important factor to keep in mind is the cost of the project. This is obviously important since you are asking for funding. Even the most well-intentioned projects may be too costly to implement effectively. Also keep in mind the benefits of starting small and working your way up to larger projects, particularly if you are new to grant writing and grant administration. If you are concerned that a larger issue will not be addressed if you start small, the flip side of this is that if you need to start small to get your feet wet. You will be able to create and manage a better program for the other need when you reach that point.

All grantors require that you prepare a budget and keep your funder updated on project costs. Even if a grantor does not specifically mention the budget requirement (and yes, some fail to do so), you need to include one anyway. It will not look good if you are too far over or under budget. Funders are sensitive to this. Similarly, using your funds in an efficient manner is important. Say you plan to create a brochure for students relating potential income of students with a high school diploma compared to those who drop out early. Creating an expensive, glossy brochure through a printing company when you could use lower-grade but nice looking paper through a local copier could give the impression that you are not cost-conscious. Do your best to create an affordable project that will yield the results you are seeking. If you or your team is hesitant about your ability to do this, begin by targeting smaller grants to both gain experience and to prove yourself to current and future grantors.

Additional Support

In addition to finding potential partnerships within your community, it is wise to obtain support from a variety of other sources. The more people behind your project, the better. People tend to work harder for something they feel personally attached to, and when it comes to making your grant a success, the more support the better. As you work to obtain support in your school and community, relate how the project will benefit the groups you are talking with. For example, your school administrator will have a different perspective on what is important than will the parents in your community.

When seeking support, think of your school's faculty and administration. Everyone is busy, and you may find people feeling there is not enough time to conduct grant research and write the proposal. These are valid concerns. This is where your grant committee will come in handy. This is also why it is important to work on your grant projects consistently throughout the year and during the slower times of the year. Parental support is also important. Your program will affect their children, so parents need to understand why the program is important, who it will help, and what your projected outcomes are from the project. Community support can be beneficial not only when developing partnerships, but also in obtaining additional materials or funding. Many grantors require that a percentage of the funds be matched by the grantee; this can be done much more easily with community support. And even though it is not directly related to grants per se, many companies prefer to support by providing material donations rather than funding. As you get involved with the community seeking support, you may find that you are better able to obtain those types of donations when you have developed those relationships.

If you plan to find matching funds or material donations, be sure to secure letters from your sources stating that they will provide the funds or items listed in the grant. Also obtain letters of commitment if you will be using a particular expert or creating a partnership with another organization or business. The letter simply needs to state that the person(s) is aware of the grant application and has agreed to provide the services listed in the proposal. If you are able to obtain letters of support from the people who will be involved in or affected by the grant, include these as well, as appendices to your proposal (you can include a footnote or other notation in your proposal narrative that these materials are available in the appropriate addendum). These can include letters from parents, staff, and even students. A letter from a student in need can be very compelling to someone reading the proposal.

Do You Really Need a Grant?

Once you have identified your need and examined your goals and objectives, ask yourself if you really need a grant. Some needs can be met by donations, volunteer time, fundraising activities, and other methods of obtaining funding. Grants are becoming more and more competitive, and they require a great deal of research and time. If you are able to meet your needs through less time intensive methods, then by all means do so!

If you feel that you might be able to meet the needs through other means, it can be well worth the time to explore those before applying for a grant, even if you feel you will end up doing so. Using the "bricks and mortar" example, you may have a very hard time obtaining a grant for construction needs, but could possibly have the materials and labor donated by a local organization or company.

Sample Grant Project Ideas

Language Arts

✧ Start an in-school or after school reading tutoring program using paid student teachers or volunteers from the community. Set up several tutoring centers in empty school classrooms and provide recent and classic fiction and nonfiction books as well as magazines, newspapers, and other media.

✧ Initiate a foreign language program. If your school does not already offer second language instruction, start a program to teach interested students. Speaking a second language and being bilingual can open many doors for students both in the personal and professional worlds. Hire a foreign language instructor or arrange for a district teacher to be paid extra to teach students in a dynamic after school setting.

✧ Provide extra English as a Second Language classes after school or at night that also invites parents of students to participate. Many times, elementary and middle school students are left to do anything in their households that involve speaking or reading English. By involving parents in ESL classes, you invest them in the work of their students and improve the home environment for the student.

✧ Replenish and update your school library by replacing damaged titles, purchasing current literature, subscribing to student and teen magazines, and updating your reference section. You might also use funds for purchasing more computers or listening stations.

✧ Direct and Improvisation Team. Hire an IMPROV director and set up an after school workshop for students. You might also use funds for purchasing props or making advertisements for performances.

✧ Foster a Book Club. Use funds to put books into the students' hands or hire a discussion leader.

Sample Grant Project Ideas

Math

✧ Train teachers to use and purchase manipulatives for the math class. Teachers might receive training from the district math coordinator, a teacher trainer from a local college, or a nationally-recognized math expert. Student knowledge could be tested with observation and standardized tests.

✧ Start an after school program that teaches students mathematics in the environment of their own community. This program could be run by teachers, aids, administrators and/or student teachers. Create math projects that focus on a problem or situation in the neighborhood surrounding the school. If possible, enlist local businesses or families to participate.

✧ Create an evening math program that includes care-givers and students. Invite students and their parents to a once a month (or once a marking period) math night that involves students and parents playing games, creating crafts, and generally having fun while "doing" math together.

✧ Initiate a school store. Use the funds to purchase a simple cash register and teach students how to operate. Students can practice using money, making transactions, buying, selling, pricing, and more. Have the students create projects or collect donations from the community.

✧ Start a competitive math after-school program. Create teams and use the funds to hire a moderator or trainer. Students can compete to do any level of math.

Sample Grant Project Ideas

Science

✧ Start an after school program that teaches students science in the environment of their own community. This program could be run by teachers, aids, administrators and/or student teachers. Create science discovery projects that focus on a problem, situation, or unique feature in the neighborhood surrounding the school. If possible, enlist local businesses or families to participate.

✧ Create a community garden. Use school property or donated land to start a community garden that is a run by a collective made up of willing neighborhood school families. Students can be responsible for daily tending of the garden. This is a great use of after school time for students. They learn about plotting land, how plants grow, needs and wants, and cooperation.

✧ Initiate a science fair. Use funds for idea books or speakers. Invite parents to the fair.

✧ Organize a camping trip for the grade. Students learn environmental facts and about the value in preserving nature. Use the funds to rent a camp for the weekend.

✧ Start a classroom zoo. Use the funds to buy animals and food for your classroom (snakes, frogs, turtles, hamsters, etc). Students can learn about classification, life cycles, habitat, and animal habits through observation and close experiences with these animals.

Sample Grant Project Ideas

Social Studies

✧ At the beginning of the school year, set up an archaeological dig either on school property or at a local nature center (with permission, of course). Obtain a number of cinder blocks (enough to create the outline of a "primitive" structure, such as a house). Excavate a large area and lay out the cinder blocks in the outline of your building. "Plant" artifacts, such as tools, animal bones, and charred wood pieces to simulate an archaeological dig. Bury the contents of your site and have students excavate at the end of the school year. In the intervening time, teach students about archaeology and famous excavated sites.

✧ Start a multicultural program. Use funds to celebrate various community cultures throughout the year by sponsoring guest speakers and readers, family multicultural nights, and to obtain authentic props from various cultures.

✧ Create an internship program that matches interested students with community businesses. Students could work in groups at local businesses to get a feel of what it is really like to have a job and to meet community members.

Other

✧ Create a professional development library either for your school or district. Stock it with periodicals, books, and teaching aids that teachers can check out for their own professional development. Also use this area to post information regarding professional development conferences. Funds might also be allocated toward sending a certain number of teachers a year to one of these conferences.

✧ Start an after school program for art or music. This could simply be a time and place for students to listen to a variety of types of music and express their artistic abilities or it could be a school jazz choir, band, theater troupe, or art club.

✧ Initiate a technology program by providing students with current technology in school. This could range from equipping every student with a working state-of-the-art calculator to providing each student with a laptop for his or her personal use. Remember that technology initiatives must have educational outcomes tied to them. Grant funders will want to know how use of the new technology will enhance the learning of your students.

✧ Replace old and peeling playground equipment. Raise funds and/or receive a grant to replace old and dangerous playground equipment, resurface play areas with kid-safe materials, and purchase outdoor equipment, such as balls, jump ropes, and sidewalk chalk.

✧ Participate in the Presidential fitness challenge. Use funds to purchase indoor and outdoor fitness equipment and/or to start an after school exercise club for students, teachers, and parents.

Chapter Two: Grants and Funders

Once you have an idea of your program, goals and objectives, you will need to begin researching funders who may be appropriate for your project. First, let's look at the types of grants you may end up considering.

Project or Program Grants

These are the most common and are exactly as they sound; they are for specific projects with a beginning and an end. Funders like these types of grants because they are limited by time and are able to demonstrate accomplishments during that timeframe. These types of grants are very common for the educational setting.

Operations Grants

These cover general operating costs. These types of grants are rare and more difficult to obtain because they are used to cover costs of conducting business; nothing new is created with this grant. These are less likely to be applied to the school setting.

Capital or Construction Grants

These are the "bricks and mortar" grants used for construction of new buildings or additions. Sometimes these are given prior to a project grant (that will take place in the new building), but there are funders who only support these types of grants.

Challenge Grants

These support part of a project; you are required to find additional funders or raise the additional funds. For those who have no or limited history in conducting projects or managing grants, these may be a good way to begin to prove yourselves. Bear in mind that this type of grant (as with most) has specific requirements on how and where you need to raise the additional funds. More and more, challenge or "matching" grants are becoming more common as funds are tight and competition is high.

Types of Funders

Let's look at the different types of funders. Grantors fall into two categories, private and public. Private funders include foundations, corporations, and private entities. Public funding comes through the government. As a grant-seeker for at-risk populations, you will likely be looking into both private and government funds, particularly those available through the Department of Education. Never rule out a source of funding. To say that a school should only apply for public grants is to miss out on a huge potential for funding. What are the differences between the various types of funders?

Public Grants

Public grants include federal, state, county, and city grant monies, and all require forms be filled out when applying for a grant. Before you get too excited about a federal grant, check the eligibility requirements. The good news here is that many federal funds are reserved for schools working on projects that address the No Child Left Behind Act. Many programs geared toward at-risk students will meet these needs. Be wary of creating a project geared toward NCLB simply to try to obtain funding—a real need has to exist and be proven through careful research and by providing data to support the claim. Most grants are now research-based, meaning that the proof you submit addressing the need has to be based on solid scientific research rather than opinion or personal experience.

Not sure if your program is a match? It is okay to call the agency to ask questions about the requirements and to clarify any confusing guidelines or directions. Just do not expect the person on the other end of the phone to tell you whether or not your project is indeed a perfect fit, sounds like a good idea, or if they think it will likely be funded. All agencies, government ones in particular, need to be fair and treat all callers equally. Do not expect or ask for any special treatment, no matter how fabulous your project. Neither should you make the mistake of asking that the guidelines be changed to meet your needs. This simply will not happen, and the request reflects poor judgment. But yes, people in the past have made this mistake.

Public grant applications are form-based, meaning that you will have to fill out preexisting forms rather than writing the grant and submitting it as a narrative. This is both helpful and not. The good news is that you do not have to create a complete proposal. But because you have limited space on applications, you need to be careful about your word choice and only include information that is pertinent to your application and that conveys the heart of your idea. There is no room for long explanations.

Public funds may also be available for staffing and training grants. The No Child Left Behind act places emphasis on quality instruction. These grants can be a good source for funds to improve staffing and pay for necessary continuing education or specialized training needed to service certain at-risk populations.

Information on federal funds can be found online at the Catalog of Federal and Domestic Assistance Web site at *www.cfda.gov*. Perhaps one of the most important federal resources you will want to research is the U.S. Department of Education (*www.ed.gov*).

Directions for government grants can be quite complicated. Give yourself plenty of time to review the instructions and compile your application. You must carefully follow all instructions. Read them a few times before beginning. On the bright side, with federal grants, you can call and ask questions as needed. You also have the opportunity to get feedback on your application if your project is rejected by calling and requesting evaluator comments. This information is highly valuable for making changes to your next application.

In addition to applying for project grants, you will also want to get on mailing lists for various organizations to be notified of Requests for Proposals, or RFPs. These requests are made available when grant monies are available for specific purposes. If your needs match or are similar to an RFP notice, take advantage and apply for the grant. You may need to alter your original idea somewhat, but if the primary purpose remains the same and will help your students, the changes can be worth it if it leads to funding.

One primary difference between federal grants and those from foundations is that federal monies typically come after the program is finished, or at specified intervals throughout the project. If you are unable to complete the project without the money up front, then foundations or other sources may be the best options. Foundation funds are often provided upfront.

Another concern with federal grants is that detailed record-keeping is an absolute must. Public grantors are much more stringent in tracking requirements including project progress, staffing, and budgeting. Any deviations from the original proposal are often required in writing for government grants, even if it is a small change. Detailed research on the population affected by the project will be required as well, including specific demographic information. Federal funds are often awarded based on statistics more so than the project. You could have a great project planned, but if the "wrong" group is affected, then the grant may not be awarded. On the other hand, at-risk students are a "hot topic" population, and a quality program that can serve this demographic and be a model for other programs stands a better chance of obtaining funding. Of course, this does not mean that you should attempt to create a program based on these factors simply to obtain funding. Addressing a real need is always the purpose of a grant.

How do you know if a federal grant is right for you? Federal grants are good choices for projects requiring larger amounts of funds, such as those over $100,000. Federal grants are also extremely competitive. If you have a very unique program, a federal grant may be a good choice. The feds also offer a number of educational grants. If you are developing a smaller project, you may want to consider seeking foundation or corporate funders first and work toward developing a grant history. A good track record will help your chances of obtaining federal funds.

Private Foundation Grants

Many types of foundations exist; thousands, actually. Foundations may have support staff and a board of directors or be simply a trust. Depending on the foundation, staff may be available to help you or to answer questions. These larger foundations will usually publish guidelines, particularly because they have specific goals in mind for what they will and will not fund. But of course, not all foundations do this, which requires more research on your part. Foundation grants are competitive grants and good options for programs under the $100,000 mark. A larger foundation may support multi-year projects, but typically these grants are for one-year periods. Foundations range in size from very large international organizations to small family-run trusts.

National Foundations

These foundations are usually large and prefer to fund projects that have impact on a broad or national level. They tend to publish guidelines and what they support can vary from broad categories to specific areas. When conducting your research, particularly for those listing broad categories, find out what they have funded in the past. Even if a funder claims to support education, for example, if they have only funded medical projects in recent years, chances are slimmer that they will support an educational project. What they say and what they do can be different, so your research needs to find out what they do. (This is true for all funders.)

Community Foundations

In contrast, community foundations are set-up to distribute funds for a variety of grantors. They are designed to support the communities in which they were created and as such, represent a wide range of possibilities. These can be a good choice for those new to the grant process.

Family Foundations

As the title suggests, these foundations are set-up by families and represent a large portion of foundations. Often these foundations will support projects meaningful to the family or to the individual who started the foundation. These grants are typically smaller (under $5,000), but this is not always the case. Family foundations are less likely to have paid staff or published guidelines so you need to do additional research to determine how to apply.

Special Interest Foundations

These foundations are designed to support very specific areas. These foundations typically only support the special interest and may also be a source of information on the topic. For example, a special interest foundation may be established to support cancer research and to provide information to the public on cancer education.

Operating Foundations

These foundations typically exist to fund specific research or programs. The foundation is set-up to support the cause or interest. Occasionally these foundations will fund outside grants, but they are not a major funding source. The most important factor when considering an operating foundation is whether or not your project is directly related to the interests of the foundation.

Private Corporate Grants

Corporate foundations are sometimes established by large companies to support the business's charitable programs. Grants from corporations are generally not very large, but can be a potential source for monies and are an excellent source to target for equipment. (If you are in need of equipment or supplies, check to see if the company has a separate contributions office; this may be the office to target rather than seeking a grant.) Corporations tend to give grants in communities where they do business. They also tend to support programs or projects that are in line with the company's mission. Similarly, corporations may be more likely to support programs that are important to their employees.

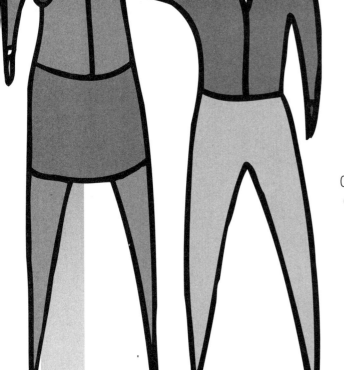

Corporate grants often do not require the stringent reporting requirements that some foundations do; however, you will likely be asked to give credit to the grantor. This can be a win-win situation for both parties; you get the funds you need to do some good and the company receives some positive PR.

The really good news is that corporations like to sponsor educational programs. The options are varied; some will provide complete grants, while others prefer partial sponsorship, matching donations, or equipment donations. When researching corporations, look for those that operate on a national level or those companies that have a strong presence in your community. Try to determine what types of programs the company has funded in the past. Many provide this information on their Web sites. You can also learn more about public companies by visiting the Securities and Exchange Commission Web site (*www.sec.gov*).

The Council for the Advancement and Support of Education (CASE) provides information on corporate matching programs and gifting prospects on their Web site at *www.case.org*.

Other Private Grants

Some wealthy individuals will be willing to support projects in the form of a grant (as opposed to a direct donation that is typically given for fundraising activities). These individuals often do not have a formal application process (although sometimes they do); in cases like this, consider submitting a short proposal or a letter of interest covering the major parts of your project. The person may then request further information in the form of an official proposal.

Researching Funders

Does the idea of searching for a funder seem a little overwhelming? The truth is that researching funders does take concentrated effort and a lot of cross-referencing of information. Why so much work? You significantly increase your chances of obtaining funding when you target funders who have historically given grants in areas similar to your project, give grants in the dollar range that you are seeking, and who have missions similar to yours. One of your first stops on the funder search is the information provided on guidelines. Certain restrictions will automatically rule out a funder, such as geographic restrictions. If a funder only supports projects in New Jersey and you live in Florida, there is no point in reading further.

One mistake is to automatically rule out a particular funder because you believe that they will not support your project for whatever reason. The funder may appear too large or too small, they give grants that are too large or too small, they only accept solicited proposals… the reasons go on. It is to your advantage to keep all your options open until after you have conducted a thorough research effort.

How you contact funders will vary. As you do your research, pay particular attention to how and when they receive applications. Some proposals, such as those for mini-grants, may only be accepted electronically. Some only accept proposals during certain months of the year or will list specific deadlines. Others publish requests for proposals (RFPs) requesting proposals for projects of a specified type. Others will accept proposals year round. If you are seeking funds from an individual donor, you may find yourself sending a "cold call" letter asking if the person would be willing to review a formal proposal. Again, keep all options open, but make special note of deadlines to give yourself plenty of time to submit your materials early (some funders will let you know if you need to supply additional information or will recommend changes—you can only take advantage of this if you get your proposal in prior to the deadline).

Foundations must file a 990-PF IRS informational return. You can learn a lot about a funder from the information submitted to the IRS, such as salaries, assets, a list of trustees, and a list of all grants given during the year. Refer to *www.guidestar.org* for researching 990-PF information.

As you conduct your research, think of the following:

◇ What types of projects does this funder typically support? (Some funders have this information listed; others do not.)

◇ Does the funder have a similar philosophy as you?

◇ Does this funder support projects of similar size and scope?

◇ Does the funder have geographical or other limitations?

◇ Does the funder require you to find other funding?

◇ What types of requirements does the funder list? Can you meet those requirements?

It can get a little discouraging when researching funders and realizing how limited some of the requirements are. This is a good thing! Each funder that does not match your program exactly is an opportunity to narrow down the field until you do find the best match. Each funder you cross off your list takes you one step closer to the one who will support your program.

Once you have determined a few of the best funders, have the committee sit down together and prioritize them into the top four or five. These are the ones for whom you will prepare proposals.

Researching Public (Government) Grants

Name of Grant	Type	Target Population	Size	Deadline	Rating 1–10	Contact

0-7682-3078-0 *Grant Writing Made Easy*

Researching Private Funders

National Foundations

Name of Funder	Restrictions	Deadlines	Target	Population Size	Rating 1-10	Contact

Community Foundations

Name of Funder	Restrictions	Deadlines	Target	Population Size	Rating 1-10	Contact

Researching Private Funders

Family Foundations

Name of Funder	Restrictions	Deadlines	Target Population	Size	Rating 1-10	Contact

Special Interest Foundations

Name of Funder	Restrictions	Deadlines	Target Population	Size	Rating 1-10	Contact

Operating Foundations

Name of Funder	Restrictions	Deadlines	Target Population	Size	Rating 1-10	Contact

Researching Private Funders

Private Corporate Grants

Name of Funder	Restrictions	Deadlines	Target Population	Size	Rating 1-10	Contact

Other Private Grants

Name of Funder	Restrictions	Deadlines	Target Population	Size	Rating 1-10	Contact

Researching Tips

Put yourself on mailing lists. Many public agencies maintain mailing lists of organizations who are interested in being notified when RFPs are published. Contact federal, state, and local agencies to be put on the lists.

As you find funding sources that look promising, do a quick check of the guidelines before getting too excited. Some eligibility issues include:

- ◇ required matching funds

- ◇ geographic restrictions

- ◇ demographic requirements

- ◇ size of grants available

- ◇ length of time allowed for project

- ◇ deadline for submission

Review as many different databases as possible (see the lists on pages 37–40). As you do your research, use a variety of keywords to conduct your search. You may find a suitable funder under a different subject heading than you might originally think. Look through the subject guides to help kick-start your thinking on headings that may have appropriate listings. Also note that most of the databases have multiple methods for conducting searches, such as subject indexes and founder indexes. Use these indexes to make your search more efficient. If you are just beginning, the subject index is a good place to start, using a variety of terms that relate to your project. If you are cross checking funder information, the funder index is obviously a better choice. You can also look up information by type of funder. Foundations and corporations are typically listed together, while public grantors are listed separately. In other words, most guides differentiate between public and private funders.

Use your local library! Many libraries maintain a large section of grant seeking materials. Also take advantage of the reference librarians; they are there to provide assistance, so ask for it. While the librarian will not sit down and look through all the materials with you, he or she will very likely help you determine the best sources to begin your search. The librarian can also point you in the direction of sources you may not think to use. Also watch for public seminars on grant seeking. Many libraries offer periodic training on grant seeking and writing, and best of all, they are free! The more information you have at your disposal, the better your chances of finding the perfect funder for your project. And the more you know about grant writing in general, the better you will be at writing one.

Do not rely solely on the Internet, but use it extensively. Many funders have their own web pages that provide much more information than their listings in directories. Many will use a *.org* address; government funders will likely use a *.gov* address. Keep in mind that anyone can create a Web site. Do not rely on any one source for your research, particularly the

Internet. Verify any funders that look suspicious or that you cannot find in any other source. Many invaluable search tools are available online, such as many Foundation Directory databases. There are also many Web sites devoted to grant writing (you will quickly get a feel for which ones are more useful than others). In today's world, the Internet is a convenient tool with a wealth of information. But keep in mind that not everything is on the Internet. You will want to use old-fashioned print sources (if they are available) such as books and newsletters in addition to electronic sources including CD-ROMS and the Internet.

In all of your searches, seek out the most current information possible. Many Web sites list a date of when the site was last updated, or at the very least, a date of when it was created. If no dates are listed, you may get a feel for how current it is by the type of information listed. Sites that reference an event that took place over a year ago may not have been updated in quite some time, and the information posted may no longer be current. With print resources, only use ones that are recent. If possible, do not use any that are older than a year. Things change quickly, and funders may change what they prefer to support from one year to the next. Always call the funder for current guidelines if you cannot determine if the information you have is up to date.

Sources

The information that follows contains some of the most commonly-used and comprehensive search methods. This list is no where near exhaustive. It is highly recommended that you visit the local library and conduct your own searches in order to find as many possible funders as you can. Do not neglect possible networking opportunities or "word of mouth" options. Sometimes the best funder may come to you from the least expected of sources, so keep your eyes and ears open. If appropriate, put the word out that you are developing a project and seeking funding. Your search for a funder is very much like a search for a job.

The Foundation Center will be one of your most important resources. It is a national organization founded and supported by various foundations. It provides information on foundations and corporate giving. The foundation offers a number of databases and publishes a wide variety of sources. Check your local library to see which ones it carries.

There are five main Foundation Center libraries throughout the United States.

Headquarters

NEW YORK
79 Fifth Avenue/16th Street
New York, NY 10003-3076
Tel: 212-620-4230
www.fdncenter.org
New York Library home page: *www.fdncenter.org/newyork*

Field Offices

ATLANTA
50 Hurt Plaza, Suite 150
Atlanta, GA 30303-2914
404-880-0094
Atlanta Library home page: *www.fdncenter.org/atlanta*

CLEVELAND
1422 Euclid Avenue, Suite 1600
Cleveland, OH 44115-2001
216-861-1934
Cleveland Library home page: *www.fdncenter.org/cleveland*

SAN FRANCISCO
312 Sutter Street, Suite 606
San Francisco, CA 94108-4314
415-397-0902
San Francisco Library home page: *www.fdncenter.org/sanfrancisco*

WASHINGTON
1627 K Street, NW, Third Floor
Washington, DC 20006-1708
202-331-1400
Washington, D.C., Library home page: *www.fdncenter.org/washington*

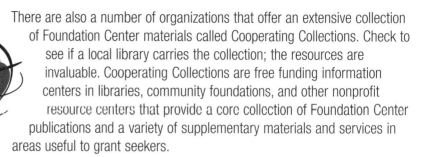

There are also a number of organizations that offer an extensive collection of Foundation Center materials called Cooperating Collections. Check to see if a local library carries the collection; the resources are invaluable. Cooperating Collections are free funding information centers in libraries, community foundations, and other nonprofit resource centers that provide a core collection of Foundation Center publications and a variety of supplementary materials and services in areas useful to grant seekers.

Lists of locations across the U.S. can be found at *www.fdncenter.org/collections*.

The Foundation Center offers numerous online directory subscription plans if you are not near a Foundation library or a Cooperating Collection. (If your local library does not carry a Cooperating Collection, consider writing a grant to fund the collection.) Subscriptions range in price depending on the directory. You can find more information at the Foundation's Web site at *www.fdncenter.org*.

Other Resources

Government

Catalog of Federal Domestic Assistance (CFDA)
print or online at *http://www.cfda.gov*

Commerce Business Daily
print or online at *http://cbdnet.gpo.gov*

Federal Grants Management Handbook
print: Thompson Publishing Group; order online at *http://www.thompson.com*

The United States Government Manual
print or online at *http://www.gpoaccess.gov*

U.S. Department of Education
http://www.ed.gov

Grants.gov
http://www.grants.gov

"Catalog of Federal Education Grants"
monthly catalog is available at an annual subscription rate of $200. For subscription information, call 1-800-655-5597.

GovSpot
links to state agencies available online at *hhtp://www.govspot.com*

Foundations

Foundation Center's Database (print and CD ROM)

The Foundation Directory

(The Foundation Center produces a number of print and electronic resources; refer to the Web site homepage at *http://www.fdncenter.org* and the library for additional sources.)

See also by the Foundation Center:

- ✧ Grants for Elementary and Secondary Education
- ✧ Grants for Children and Youth
- ✧ Grants for Community/Economic Development, Housing, and Employment
- ✧ Grants for Arts, Culture, and the Humanities
- ✧ Grants for Human/Civil Rights
- ✧ Grants for Libraries and Information Services
- ✧ Grants for Literacy, Reading, and Adult/Continuing Education
- ✧ Grants for Matching and Challenge Support
- ✧ Grants for Mental Health, Addictions, and Crisis Services
- ✧ Grants for Minorities
- ✧ Grants for Physically and Mentally Disabled
- ✧ Grants for Program Evaluation
- ✧ Grants for Science and Technology Programs
- ✧ Grants for Social and Political Science Programs
- ✧ Grants for Social Services
- ✧ Grants for Women and Girls

The Council on Foundations
http://www.cof.org

Corporate

The Foundation Center's Directory of Corporate Giving
http://www.fdncenter.org

Council for the Advancement and Support of Education (CASE)
information on corporate matching programs online at *http://www.case.org*

Educational and Miscellaneous

"Education Grants Alert"
information on K–12 funding; report published 50 times a year at a subscription rate of $299. Call 1-800-655-5597.

"The Grantwriter's Newsletter of Funding Resources"
grant sources and contests. $36 for 12 issues. 617 Wright Avenue, Terrytown, LA 70056.

GuideStar
national database of nonprofit organizations; *http://www.guidestar.org*

National Center for Charitable Statistics
http://nccsdataweb.urban.org

Directory of Education Grants
(Research Grant Guides)

Funding Sources for K–12 Schools and Adult Basic Education
(Oryx Press)

Guide to Federal Funding for Education
(Educational Funding Research Council; subscription; see library resources)

National Guide to Funding for Elementary and Secondary Education
(The Foundation Center)

DIALOG comprehensive search tool
online at *http://www.dialog.com* or through local library if available

GrantStation
http://www.grantstation.com

The Giving Forum
http://www.givingforum.com

"Chronicle of Philanthropy"
nonprofit newspaper, online at *http://www.philanthropy.com*

"Nonprofit Times"
articles for nonprofits, online at *http://www.nptimes.com*

Courting Prospective Funders

Just as you would network in a job search, so also do you network prospective funders. When you have narrowed down your choices, you may want to contact the funders prior to submitting a formal proposal. There are various ways of doing this.

When approaching a new funder about whom you know nothing, a letter of introduction can be an effective tool. For a letter of introduction, send your letter to a specific individual and inform the recipient of who you are, the school you represent, and your mission and goals.

After you have introduced yourself, you can add funders to your list of people and organizations to whom you send your newsletters and other publicity information—just be sure to include a letter with the first mailing, explaining that this newsletter is designed to keep the public informed of progress and activities at your school. If you have the time and personnel, you can even create a newsletter that you send only to your prospective funders. This list does not need to be limited only to the four or five you will first target; however, you do not want to spam a huge list of grantors, either. Pick the ones you would most like to be involved with over the next few years.

When sending newsletters or related information, be sure to obtain the name of a person within the organization to whom you can address the letter. Mail addressed to the organization without a contact name is much more likely to end up in the recycle bin. Once you have developed a solid mailing list, you can also use it to keep funders apprised of your projects and grant success. As you manage grant programs, share the news of the success! Give credit to your funders (unless they ask to remain anonymous) and let the recipients know the results of the program. You can also use this list when you have important events to publicize (such as faculty or school awards, presentations, etc.), press releases, or newspaper clippings about your school or faculty.

The query letter can be used after you have made initial contact with a funder. This letter is designed to gather information from the funder about their programs and to request guidelines. Explain your project briefly; explaining that from the research you have conducted, it looks like you may be a good match. If appropriate, you may also ask for a meeting to discuss your program. Remember, you want to ensure that you are targeting an appropriate funder before creating a full proposal. For some larger or innovative programs, it may be worth everyone's time to discuss the project first.

You can also contact the funders by phone for the same information you are seeking in the query. Be prepared when you make the call. If you do not have all your information in front of you and a list of questions, you may forget to mention important points. Again, try to obtain the name of a specific person before making the call; otherwise, you may need to make a couple of calls to first determine the best person for you to talk to about your project. Remember, everyone is busy; always respect the time of the people you call. It may be best to try to schedule a phone interview. As long as you are clear about the reason for your call (seeking information or to clarify rules) and are professional, many people will be willing to talk if their schedules allow. If you call only to pitch your program and ask for money, you will not make a good impression.

If someone on your faculty or on your board knows someone in a funding organization, take advantage of the connection if it is appropriate. This may require a bit of judgment. For example, some organizations may allow their board members to support programs that are generally out of the funder's areas of interest; you may run across this situation. If there is a personal contact within an organization that does support your type of project, then by all means use the contact, but always remain professional.

Remember when you are contacting funders before submitting a proposal that you are not yet asking for funding—you are asking for information. Naturally, discussions about your project will occur, but keep these geared towards determining if there is a good match with the funder and if your project meets their guidelines. Think of all contact with funders as opportunities to cultivate relationships rather than simply a means to an end.

Sometimes funders will sponsor events to discuss their funding projects and discuss grant writing issues. There may also be an opportunity to meet with the organization's representatives to discuss potential projects. If one of these events is taking place in your area, make plans to attend. Even if the organization is not one you would normally consider approaching, attending the event could be productive given the type of information presented on the grants process.

Sample Query Letter

Always send grant-related correspondence on your school or organization letterhead.

 Middleville Elementary School

Jane Doe
Chairperson, Grant Committee
Calculator Corporation
1234 Charity Way
New York, NY 11111

January 1, 2010

Dear Ms. Doe,

Our department of curriculum has developed an exciting new after school program to use calculators to teach graphing and data analysis skills to students in grades 5–6. This promising program will give underprivileged students access to innovative technology and supply them with the skills necessary to succeed in the twenty-first century.

From our research, it appears that your company pursues similar goals. I am writing to request information regarding your grant programs and to request guidelines and submission deadlines. If you should require further information regarding our program please contact me via telephone, e-mail, or mail, using the information below.

Thank you very much for your time. I will await further word from you.

Sincerely,

John Doe

John Doe
Fifth Grade Teacher
E-mail: jdoe@k12.com
Phone: 111-111-1111

567 Main Street ● Chicago ● Illinois ● 22222

 0-7682-3078-0 *Grant Writing Made Easy*

Networking List

Maintain a list of all people you meet in your quest for grant-writing gold. Keep all names, contact information, and relevant information in one location.

Name	Organization	Address	Grant Interest Area	Circumstances of First Meeting	Date Last Contacted	Other

0-7682-3078-0 *Grant Writing Made Easy*

Networking Opportunities

The following is a list of events where you might be able to make strategic contacts in for your grant-writing efforts. Add your own ideas to the list.

Event	Date	Location	Significance
ASCD Convention	March	varies	Association for Supervision and Curriculum Development national show attracts superintendents, curriculum developers researchers, educational speakers, educators, and education companies
IRA Convention	1st week in May	varies	International Reading Association national show attracts well-known literary figures, educational speakers, educators, and education companies
NAEYC Convention	November	varies	National Association for the Education of Young Children national show attracts early childhood educators, day care companies, educators, and education companies
NCSS Convention	November	varies	National Council for Social Studies national show attracts educational speakers, educators, and education companies
NCTM Convention	1st week in April	varies	National Council of Teachers of Mathematics national show attracts educational speakers, educators, and education companies
NSTA Convention	April	varies	National Science Teachers Association national show attracts educational speakers, educators, and education companies

Chapter Three: Writing the Grant

Even though each grant you write will be tailored to the specific funder you are targeting, this section will review the basic elements of a grant. Some funders will require longer or shorter sections, or may not require each section. Being capable of preparing each section is necessary, however, to be able to develop any type of grant. Always include a needs statement, list of goals and objectives, and a budget in some form, even if not specifically mentioned by the funder.

In general, a grant consists of a narrative and a budget. The narrative is broken down into a variety of sections. The budget details exactly how the money requested will be spent and refers directly to the information presented in the narrative. Sometimes the budget will also have its own separate narrative. Additional information such as resumes of staff involved and other supporting documents may be included in appendices. Items you will need to address in the grant include a number of key elements.

What is the point of the project? You need to have a clear idea of why you are doing the project and who it will help. Can you summarize the purpose in a few sentences? If not, you may need to revisit the project to narrow it down to the key points. Larger projects will, of course, have a broader vision; however, the program should not be so complicated that it cannot be summarized briefly. If you are unable to do this, the project may not yet be focused enough.

How will it happen? Who will do what? Knowing the primary activities of the project is essential. Your funder will need to know exactly what their money will be supporting. Be prepared to alter the project if necessary to meet the needs of the funder. Also be clear about who will be doing what. You will be providing a list of needed personnel and their roles.

What will happen if you do not receive funding? Examine whether you will continue by scaling down the project or whether it will fall through. And what about the flip side of this? If you do receive funding, will you be able to carry on the project after your scheduled completion date?

How will you know if you succeeded? Having a clear idea of the methods you will use to evaluate your program is needed to determine who you helped and by how much. You will need to provide a report to your funder on the success (or failure) of the project.

The Importance of Teachers

When seeking educational grants, remember that teachers are very important in the process. Teachers must be involved and must be stakeholders in the project. One or two teachers are not enough to carry a grant successfully in the school setting. Multiple teachers need to be involved, and commitment to the project needs to be obtained before a grant is developed. Use your grant committee to help involve teachers and inform those who are not directly involved in the grant writing and developing process. Explain the importance of the project and the projected outcomes. Also consider developing a culture that encourages grant ideas. In the downtimes, encourage personnel to be thinking of and making notes for future grant projects. These can be reviewed and discussed by the formal grant committee.

Parts of a Grant

Although the order of some elements may vary, a general outline of a grant includes the following.

Abstract of Project: A brief overview of the project

Included in the Narrative

Title: The name of the project

Project Summary: Introduces the project (also referred to as Summary of Project, Project Description, Project Overview, Discussion of Project, etc.)

Statement of Need: Detailed information on why the project should be funded (also referred to as Problem Area, Justification, Rationale, Critical Impact Statement, Definition of Need, Defense, or Assessment)

Goals and Objectives: Goals of the project and how they will be met

Project Methods (Activities): Methods used to meet objectives

Timetables: Total length of project, including essential milestones

Evaluation of Program: How outcomes of project will be evaluated

Dissemination, Utilization, and Sustainability: Sharing results with others and continuation of project

Budget: Detailed outline of expenses

Other Items That May be Included in the Narrative or in the Addenda

Facilities and Equipment: What is needed and where the project will take place

Personnel: Who will be involved in the project and their qualifications

The Abstract

The abstract is a concise overview of the project; often only a paragraph or two. A quality abstract is vital because it may be the only part of your proposal that some reviewers see in the initial phase of reviewing applications. Obviously, it is an important element of the proposal. Most grant writers recommend writing the abstract last. This is because the process of completing all other elements of the proposal will give the writer a solid feel for the proposal and what parts should be emphasized in the abstract to best summarize the project. The abstract should touch on each major element of the proposal. The abstract can also be used for gaining community support and in promoting the project.

The Title

Some people recommend a catchy title. How much this helps is debatable and not all grant writers agree on the best approach. What you do want to aim for in the title is one that will portray the essence of the grant and make the reader want to learn more, but not be too cute or flashy that it is a turnoff. In other words, a less flashy, but more informative title is preferred to one that is catchy but means nothing to the person reading it. The title used may also vary from grant to grant depending on the funder. Tailor the title to appeal to the funder's priorities. A corporate foundation may appreciate a flashier title while a government agency will likely prefer a straightforward title. When in doubt, opt for conservative over flashy. Also strive to keep the title short. When composing the title, think about the end result of the program and incorporate this into the title. You want your reader to get an immediate feel for the purpose of the program and want to read more.

Project Summary

This is the introduction to the narrative of your grant. Here is the place where you want to draw your reader in and compel him or her to read more. How do you do this? Take advice from journalists and writers of articles. Think about how magazines do this: they use "hooks" throughout to make the reader want to continue. On the cover is a short, compelling title that grabs your attention. Inside, you find the longer version of the title, which leads you to the correct page. How do most articles begin? With a startling statistic, an appealing quote, a personal story, an interesting anecdote, or any other method of immediately garnering interest. These introductions draw you into the article, making you want to read more.

Following this brief hook, the writer often moves immediately into the heart of the issue, explaining the situation and why it is a problem. Then the rest of the article continues, often citing expert opinions, providing graphs or other data, additional statistics, methods that have been used to solve the problem or to try and solve it, what has worked and what has not... the list goes on.

Because the introduction is likely the place where you will begin writing, consider grabbing a few magazines and reading some articles to get a feel for developing a strong hook. This can also help free up your creative juices if you are feeling the stress of a common malady among writers… writer's block. In case this is an issue, another good reason for beginning with the project summary is because this is the place where you can let your passion for the need and the project shine through. It is the reason you are seeking a grant in the first place.

Use these writing tools and stress the need for the project (in brief terms), who will be affected, and how. What will happen if the project is funded? How will lives be changed? Play to the reader's emotions without going over the top. Present the facts, but in a manner that shows the human side of the issue, not just the statistics (these will be presented later). Help your reader feel the same passion for your students and the project that you do.

The introduction should include some other essential information. It introduces your school to the funder. Include a brief history of the school to give the funder an idea of who you are, what you do, and a general idea of the types of students you serve. If the school has achieved any major accomplishments, note this in the introduction. Have you already implemented a successful program addressing other issues? What types of activities are already in place? Also make note of any existing relationships with the community and the support system in place for the project.

Statement of Need

Why should a grantor give your project funds? Why is the project needed? Who will be served? The statement of need shows the funder, in specific ways, who will be affected by your project and why it is needed. The statement should convince the funder of the importance of the project. How do you do this?

Think back to the magazine article example. Imagine an article on breast cancer arguing the need for continuing funds to fight the disease and to promote education. An article like this would likely open with a story along the following lines:

> A young woman who had no family history of the disease found a lump in her breast. Because of her age and family history, she ignored it for a while. At her yearly doctor appointment, she casually mentioned it to her doctor, who immediately sent her for a mammogram. The test showed she had fourth-stage cancer and further tests showed it had spread to her lymph nodes.

This article would, of course, present the information in a much more personal tone. The reader would learn about her personal life and how she had to drop out of law school to go in for treatment. She ended up moving back in with her parents because she did not have insurance.

When seeking grant funds, the whole purpose is to serve a population that needs something. Help. Assistance. Support. In your case, you have a group of students who are not excelling for whatever reason. But why should your funder care? Almost every school in the nation could make a case for a group of students who are not receiving the assistance they need to excel. You need to show the need. There is a saying in writing circles that says, "Show, don't tell." What this means is that, rather than telling the reader that a character is angry, show it through the character's words and actions.

Take some tips from journalists and fiction writers. Review those articles again. Read a good fiction book in your spare time. How do the writers show the emotions and struggles of their subjects? This is what you will need to do, to some extent, in the needs statement and throughout your proposal. To what extent varies among grant writers, but you definitely need to show your reader, in both your words and your supporting data what the needs of your students are, how the lack of these needs affects them, and what will happen or continue to happen if you do not receive funds to carry-out this project. Use the personal touch. Help your reader feel for your students. Speak to the reader's emotions. It reminds everyone of why you are applying for the grant: because real people are facing real problems. It can be easy to get lost in the data. Use your narrative to speak to the human side of the issue.

If your project is modeled after another successful program, show the results of the original program. Use specific numbers. How many students were affected? How did test scores improve? By how much? How many students stayed in school or took part in after school programs? Were drug or alcohol related dropouts reduced? Show that the model program was effective and that by receiving funding you can obtain the same results in your school.

For a new program, explain the problem and show how many students are expected to be served. How often does the problem affect students or staff? Have any other projects been undertaken to try and address the problem? Why is this new idea better? What will happen if the project does not take place? Will the situation remain the same or get worse? Show that there is a dire need for the project with tangible results with or without funding.

When writing the statement of need, use a variety of sources to back-up your claims and help the funder understand the importance of the project. Demographic studies can be used to show percentages of affected persons and demonstrate the need. Letters of support from parents, community members, and others involved in the project can be used to show acceptance of the idea. Choose sources that are reliable.

Take care to use information that is current within the past few years. Also put your information into context for the funder, comparing the data in your area with data in other areas with similar problems. Show that the need is greater in your community than in others using numbers as proof.

Goals and Objectives

Once the need has been established, highlight the project's goals and objectives. Again, the goals are the desired end-results of the project. Objectives are measurable means of achieving those goals. Each goal should have at least one objective. In the grant, list goals and objectives together so the reader can easily see what the goals are and how exactly you plan to reach those goals. A good way to do this is using a simple list: write the first goal, and then list each objective below it. Continue with each goal until all have been listed. Do not write your goals and objectives in narrative form as you do other parts of your grant. You want this section to be very clear and easily understood.

Bear in mind when writing goals and objectives that both speak to the desired outcomes of the project—what the end results will be. Neither goals nor objectives indicate how you plan to conduct the project. Also remember that objectives need to be measurable statements, such as "Eighty-five percent of first grade students will be able to demonstrate grade-level proficiency by the close of the project." Write your goals and objectives in a clear and concise manner and ensure the objective statement is measurable.

Take care not to list too many goals; this could be seen as poor planning. It is good to have high hopes for change, but funders may view too many goals as impractical. A project with fewer goals that can be realistically attained is better than a project that is trying to accomplish too much and is doomed for failure. A good target is to list one goal for each major problem addressed in the Statement of Need.

Objectives should be short, measurable, action-oriented, specific, and directly related to the Statement of Need and the goal under which they are listed. Because objectives need to be measurable, ensure that the objective can be evaluated to monitor progress and to complete the final assessment of the project. When writing your objectives, list who will be affected and what the results will be. For example,

"Students will improve math scores by at least one grade letter by the end of the program."

"Teachers will complete three modules of continuing education in a one-year period."

Notice that these statements contain action verbs: improve and complete. Use "power verbs" when composing your objectives. The following pages contain lists of "power verb" ideas:

Power Verbs

absorb	clarify	detail	exceed
accommodate	combine	detect	execute
accomplish	communicate	determine	exercise
achieve	compare	differentiate	exhibit
acquire	compile	discover	expand
adapt	complete	discuss	explain
analyze	compose	display	explore
answer	compute	distinguish	express
apply	connect	double	extend
approach	consider	earn	extract
arrange	construct	elaborate	fill
articulate	continue	elect	find
assimilate	contribute	elicit	form
attain	convert	employ	formulate
attend	convey	end	fulfill
avoid	cooperate	engage	function
begin	create	enlarge	further
calculate	decide	ensure	gain
categorize	define	entertain	garner
change	deliver	establish	generate
check	demonstrate	estimate	graduate
choose	describe	evaluate	grasp
cite	design	examine	group

Power Verbs (cont.)

handle	maintain	perform	reference
one	make	pinpoint	refocus
hypothesize	manipulate	place	reiterate
identify	map	play	relate
illustrate	master	present	remodel
imagine	memorize	prevail	render
improve	model	print	reorganize
improvise	modify	process	repair
incorporate	name	produce	replace
increase	narrate	progress	report
inspect	navigate	prove	represent
install	negotiate	quadruple	reproduce
integrate	observe	qualify	research
interact	obtain	question	respond
interpret	operate	raise	restore
invent	orchestrate	rate	retrieve
investigate	organize	reach	review
isolate	outline	read	revise
itemize	outperform	realize	search
judge	overcome	recognize	select
learn	own	record	shape
locate	participate	recover	share
log	pass	reduce	sharpen

Power Verbs (cont.)

shorten	transcribe	accelerate	assemble
simulate	transition	act	assess
sketch	translate	activate	assign
solve	travel	add	assist
sort	treat	address	assure
speak	trim	adjust	augment
specify	triple	administer	author
start	uncover	adopt	authorize
strengthen	undertake	advance	automate
study	upgrade	advise	award
submit	uphold	advocate	balance
succeed	use	affect	benchmark
summarize	verbalize	affirm	benefit
supply	verify	aid	bolster
surpass	visualize	alleviate	boost
sustain	voice	allocate	bridge
synthesize	weigh	allot	broaden
systemize	withstand	alter	budget
tabulate	work	appoint	build
tackle	write	appraise	capitalize
talk		approve	capture
test	**Teachers will:**	ascertain	care
total	abolish	aspire	catalogue

Power Verbs (cont.)

chronicle	correspond	embrace	formalize
circulate	counsel	emphasize	fortify
circumvent	critique	empower	forward
classify	cultivate	enable	foster
coach	customize	encourage	fund
collaborate	decrease	enforce	furnish
collect	dedicate	enhance	gather
commission	delegate	enlist	gauge
conceive	deploy	enrich	govern
conceptualize	designate	enroll	guarantee
conduct	develop	equip	guide
confer	devise	evaluate	head
configure	diagnose	expect	heighten
confirm	direct	expedite	help
conserve	dispense	experiment	hire
consolidate	disseminate	facilitate	host
consult	distribute	familiarize	ignite
contact	document	fashion	implement
contract	draft	field	incite
control	drive	finalize	include
convince	edit	fix	index
coordinate	educate	focus	individualize
correct	eliminate	forecast	influence

inform	listen	partner	purchase
infuse	manage	perceive	quantify
initiate	maximize	persuade	rally
innovate	measure	pilot	rank
inspire	mediate	pioneer	realign
instill	mentor	plan	rearrange
institute	merge	predict	reason
instruct	minimize	prepare	rebuild
insure	mobilize	prescribe	receive
intensify	moderate	preserve	recommend
intercede	mold	preside	reconcile
intervene	monitor	prevent	reconstruct
interview	motivate	prioritize	recruit
introduce	nurture	procure	rectify
inventory	offer	program	redesign
involve	officiate	project	redirect
issue	offset	promote	refer
join	open	proofread	regulate
launch	order	propose	rehabilitate
lead	orient	protect	reinforce
lecture	originate	provide	renew
lessen	overhaul	prune	reshape
lift	oversee	publicize	resolve

Power Verbs (cont.)

restructure	support	vitalize
revamp	survey	volunteer
revitalize	systematize	widen
reward	tally	yield
run	target	
safeguard	teach	
save	team	
schedule	terminate	
screen	tighten	
secure	track	
separate	trade	
serve	train	
simplify	transform	
spearhead	transmit	
specialize	troubleshoot	
sponsor	tutor	
staff	underscore	
standardize	unify	
steer	unite	
streamline	update	
structurc	urge	
suggest	utilize	
supervise	validate	

Project Methods

This is one of the largest sections of the grant proposal and describes in detail how you plan to run your project. Included in this section is a short introduction, the activities that will take place in the project, any other groups or organizations that will be involved, who will staff the project, work plans, and an overview of the end results of the project. It is the meat of the project—what will actually take place.

In addition to describing the methodologies, you will also justify why you are choosing these methods over others. Have similar programs succeeded or failed using these or other methods? Why are these methods the best choice for the number of people being served by the project? Why did you choose these activities over others? If this is a new project, why do you believe these actions are the best?

When creating this section, you need to show that these methods will be successful or are likely to produce the desired outcomes. Also show the order in which activities will take place. And wherever possible, provide evidence showing that the desired outcomes will likely occur. This evidence can come from prior programs or because the person designing the activities is an expert in the field. This section covers a range of information. Not surprisingly, it details the purpose of the program and leads into key information including the goals and objectives of the project. How will the methods used create the change desired? What are the implications of the project? How long will it take? Who will be involved?

The Introduction
The introduction to the methodology does not need to be long. It provides a brief overview of the methods that will be used and gives a summary of the format used to present the rest of the information in the methodology section.

The Activities
This section provides a detailed overview of what exactly will take place during the course of the project.

An example of activities involved in a staff development program might be:

Step 1: Off-site training #1 on use of manipulatives in reading classes

Step 2: Off-site training #2 on use of manipulatives in reading classes

Step 3: On-site classroom examination with observation by professional

Step 4: Off-site follow-up training to review best practices and compare notes

Step 5: Periodic (every 90 days) evaluation of teacher and student progress

Even if some activities seem obvious, use the opportunity to explain your methods. If the person reading the grant does not understand what will take place, or what certain "industry jargon" means, you will not be funded. Everything should be very clear to whoever reads the grant, whether that person is a potential funder, someone directly involved in the program, or people from another organization who will provide support or be involved.

Need help determining the best activities? Take time to conduct (you guessed it) research on models of similar programs that other agencies have completed. Best practices are those that have proven to be effective. Find out which programs similar to yours have had good results and model your programs after those. Try to contact the organization or program director to request a copy of the program overview or evaluation. Find out if any additional information is available, such as videos or other documentation that can help you get a feel for the original program and the best way to carry out the activities.

Personnel

In this section, each person working on the grant will be listed. Include the name of the individual (if known; if you are seeking an expert or will be hiring, list the job title only), the person's title, and what the roles and responsibilities of that person will be. Because you will likely be using current staff, make note of how much of their in-school time will be devoted to the project (this will also help you determine what to budget for compensation costs). It is expected that a certain percentage of your staff's time will be devoted to the project. Determine this percentage and list it here; include in your budget the correlating salary requirement for the project based on that percentage. Bear in mind that it will look odd to your funder if senior personnel will be spending large amounts of time on the project.

Summarize the qualifications of each key person. About a half page is usually about how much space you will have. This summarization forces you to only focus on key information directly related to the project. It may be impressive that a key resource has over 15 years experience in administering budgets, but if this person's involvement is to conduct training, of the budget information is not necessary to include. Resumes of personnel will not be included here; this information will be provided in the appendix if allowable.

Determining how many and what type of personnel are needed for the project should be considered carefully. Once you put it in writing, you must stick to it when you receive funding. If you later find that you are over- or under-staffed, this will not put you in a favorable position. Even for a first-time grant writer, there are no excuses for not conducting the best research possible to determine the resources needed for the project. Change occurs, of course, but your goal is as few changes as possible. Ideally you will run your program exactly as you said you would in the proposal.

How do you determine who will be involved in the grant? The primary personnel should have extensive experience in the type of program. Has management been involved with this type of program before? The principal? Do the teachers who will be working closely on the project have any specialized training in this area? Has enough time been allocated for each person involved to complete the project? Funders want to know that the money they will put toward the project will go to good use and be managed well. The people entrusted to running the program need to be

trustworthy and experienced. If the program is specialized, the people involved should be familiar with the specialty.

Keep in mind that the funder does not know you or your staff. While you may meet with the funders beforehand to discuss the project, in general, the funder is relying on the information you provide to convince them that your personnel are qualified. Choose your primary staff carefully and sell their history and accomplishments that are directly related to the project goals. As with other parts of the proposal, you may be limited in how much information you can provide on key personnel. Choose those outstanding accomplishments and prior work experiences that will sell the people you have lined up and that are directly related to the tasks outlined in the proposal. Include as many specific individuals as you can. A person's 20-year history running ESL programs is much more impressive than a line stating "to be hired" when describing the program manager of a literacy program.

Because a number of people will be involved in the project, be sure to list all key members and demonstrate that all stakeholders are equally represented in the project. For example, when community members are involved, their roles in the project should be of equal standing (although in different roles) to those of the teachers involved. In other words, this is a group effort and needs to be (accurately) presented that way.

Timetables

Before you begin your project, you need to have an idea of how long it will take. Is it a year-long after school program or a special two-week intensive project? Are there significant milestones (such as scheduled testing) along the way that you need to note? Your project needs to have a specific beginning and an end. Funders are not likely to fund a project that has no end in sight. For those projects that are long term and for which you have ongoing plans, you still need to mark a beginning and end. Following the "end" of the project with the targeted funder, you will need to inform your grantor how you plan to continue the project and how you plan to fund the ongoing activities (sustainability of the project).

There are a number of ways to track the timeline of a project. Some software programs allow you multiple ways to show timelines, but you do not need to use a fancy program to show your plans. It is wise to do some homework on different methods of showing your timeline. Pick one that is both most appropriate for you and because it fits the guidelines of some funders. The following is a brief list of some common tracking tools.

A PERT (Project Evaluation and Review Technique) chart is a flowchart that shows the relationship between activities. PERT charts are typically drawn by hand. The chart originates from a single point and moves "forward" through lines connecting activities. Those actions that take place at the same time are presented along the line in a vertical fashion.

Gant Charts are timeline charts that show activities across a timeline using horizontal bars to represent each activity.

Activity Calendars show activities as they take place using a standard calendar system.

Timelines can also be written out as a list in chronological order. This works best when no or few activities take place simultaneously. If many activities are taking place simultaneously, using a project management chart can be very helpful for both you and your funder. As you create your timeline, you will gain a better understanding of your project and if your projected or desired timelines are realistic.

Evaluation of Program

How will you know if your project was successful? You need to have a plan for evaluating the results of the program, both for your own records and for reporting to your grantor. Some funders are less stringent in their requirements for reporting outcomes; however, it is in your best interest to keep detailed records on the success of your project. This helps build a track record of success that you can use in your next grant application.

How specific do you need to be in your evaluation? An easy way to create your plan is to have an evaluation method for each objective you created. Because your objectives are measurable, your evaluation method should make itself known through the objective. If, for example, your objective is a decreased rate of teen pregnancies in your school district, your evaluation will consist of obtaining numbers of pregnant students before and after your program. Obviously, some results may not be immediately available. Make accommodations in your timeline to track results for a realistic period of time, or follow the funder's guidelines if they are provided.

Evaluations should consist of a few pieces of information; again, some of this will be determined by your objectives, but in general you will track: who will be evaluated, the information that will be collected to conduct the evaluation, the source(s) of information, procedures used to collect data, how the data will be analyzed, the timeline (see above), who will conduct the evaluation, and how the results will be used. Many funders require that an independent party conduct or at least review the evaluation. Read the funders' directions on this so you can tailor your proposal appropriately and make arrangements for an evaluation before you begin.

Ensure that you have access to third-party evaluators. You should never evaluate your own program. A third-party's evaluation will be much more meaningful. You may not be required to list the specific entity, but you will need to state that you have access to an evaluator; and of course, make sure this is a true statement. For federal grants, you will need to have a specific person lined up ahead of time and may be asked to include that person's name in the application. You also need to let your funder know how and when you will provide results. Some projects lend themselves to periodic reporting; others make sense to only report at the close of the project, and some may require reporting some time after the project has ended and results can be determined. And of course, the funder's requirements may be the determining factor in how and when your evaluation and reporting takes place.

0-7682-3078-0 *Grant Writing Made Easy*

You may also be able to use your state's standardized test scores from year to year as part of your evaluation method.

There is more than one way to evaluate a program, but a thorough evaluation should use a variety of evaluation methods. You should ensure that the evaluation serves the needs of the end users, that it is conducted legally, ethically, and fairly, that it is scientifically-based (meaning that the results are technically accurate and are adequate enough to find the value of the program), and that the methods are given realistic time frames, staffing, and funding.

A comprehensive evaluation will address all four components. The evaluation is an important tool not only for reporting to your funder but also in determining which parts of the project were successful and which ones could use improvement (or which ones failed, and why). As you move into the next project, what you learn from the first can be carried over. Review the evaluation results with your grant committee to determine how you can best incorporate the results.

Find outside help in creating your evaluation statements if you need it. They are an important, but potentially difficult, component of the grant. Whomever you contact to do your final evaluation can help you develop an effective evaluation plan.

Because your evaluation tools are directly related to the objectives, consider listing them with your goals and objectives in list form, such as:

Goal One:

Objective One:

Evaluation One:

Objective Two:

Evaluation Two:

Objective Three:

Evaluation Three:

This makes it very clear for your reader exactly what will take place in the program and how each activity will be evaluated. This method of listing can also be useful to you in tracking your project.

Ideally your third party evaluator will be from your community or familiar with it. If there is a local university, consider contacting the school for names of professors or retired professors with experience in your project area. If you need to hire a professional evaluator, you may be able to locate one through a local organization that supports nonprofit organizations. You can also look outside your immediate area to hire an evaluation professional through the American Association of Grant Professionals at *www.grantprofessionals.org* or by conducting an online search. If you opt for the second method, use your best judgment in reviewing sites.

Ask potential evaluators for names of organizations they have worked for in the past, and call for references. Do not be afraid to interview prospective evaluators; after all, your evaluation will not only have an effect on how your current funder sees you, but will also have an effect on your future grant seeking efforts.

> What methods will you use for evaluation?
>
> Will you be available to meet on-site with personnel and participants?
>
> How many man hours will this evaluation take and what is your hourly fee?
>
> Can you give me an estimate of costs and services before being contracted?
>
> Will you be available to give progress reports throughout the program to my board of directors or to the school board?
>
> When and how will you keep update me with progress reports?

Dissemination, Utilization, and Sustainability

Many funders, particularly government funders and those supporting public education, want to know how your project can benefit others beyond the immediate scope of the project. If you have a solid plan for sharing the results of your project it can increase your chances of obtaining funding. Dissemination is a required part of the grant process.

Dissemination involves sharing the results of your project and funder information with others and is always included in your proposal. Dissemination can take many forms, including training, workshops, presentations, or creation of written materials, public service announcements, media coverage, and publication of the funder's name or logo. Private sources, in particular, like to know that their name will be publicized and included in the marketing of the project.

Utilization includes usage of the information gained and may require more in-depth plans, also including training, presentations, workshops, or other methods to put the results of your project to use. Depending on the goals of the grant, the dissemination and utilization section may require a detailed description of your plans. Obviously, showing others how to implement results from your project will take more effort than simply sharing the outcomes of your project with others. Whatever you plan to do with the results of your project, include information on whom you will share the results with, the methods you will use, and whether or not your plans include more involved sharing of results, such as presentations.

Sustainability refers to how the project or program will continue after the grant has been used. Do you have plans to keep the program alive? (You should!) Will you be using your own funds or seeking additional grants? If you will be seeking additional funds, list possible sources so the first funder will acknowledge that you have put some thought into the future of the program. Include letters of support from school officials, other teachers, parents, and community members indicating commitment to continue the work. Funders are more willing to support a project that has ongoing commitment and plans for continuing funding.

Budget

It goes without saying that the budget is a crucial element of your proposal. After all, you are asking for money, and the funder needs to know how you plan to spend that money. All grant proposals, even the shortest ones, should include a budget. Even for grants where limited instructions are included, send a budget plan with your application.

How detailed should the budget be? This will depend somewhat on your project; however, some guidelines apply to most budgets. First, nothing should appear on the budget that is not referenced in the narrative. Of course, you will not list every single office supply, but do not try to slip in vague budget terms to purchase items that are not directly related to the project, even if your school is in desperate need of a new copier or fax machine. Be sure to read the funder's guidelines carefully; many funders will not pay for office equipment or construction, for example. Do not include anything that the funder explicitly says they will not pay for, even if you think it is vital for the program's success. You may need to seek additional funding for these items from a funder who does not cover these items or seek an in-kind gift or donation.

Items that will need to be separated out include personnel, costs of facilities (such as rent; these are known as indirect costs) and equipment specific to the project, travel costs, services, and materials and supplies specific to the project (again, do not try to "pad" this area). Essentially, all major areas of the project should be listed in the budget under separate categories. This will allow your funder to see exactly how much of the total amount requested will be going to each area. All sections and items on your budget will be discussed in some form in your narrative. This is not the place to include any surprises. You may also be asked to include or determine a need to include a separate narrative for your budget explaining items on the budget.

Be sure to read the grantor's directions on allowable and non-allowable costs. Funders vary in what they will fund. If your budget includes items for costs that are not allowable by that funder, you give yourself immediate cause for rejection. Carefully read all information from the funder on how to create the budget and what you are required to include as well as what you are not allowed to include. If you are using a standard budget to work from, remember that each funder may have different requirements and rules, and you will need to take care to make the necessary changes to each proposal's budget.

The budget is often not created by the grant writer. If needed, seek the help of someone skilled in finance, such as the school's financial administrator or outside help. This is one area where you do not want to "wing it" if you are uncomfortable creating a budget. Funders will know if the amount of funding you are requesting is reasonable given your project description. For this same reason, do not attempt to pad or inflate the budget or sneak in anything not directly related to the project. It is unethical and will reflect poorly on you. Think about it: This is what funders do. While you may end up writing many grants in your lifetime, funders will review many more. They know when someone is attempting to "pull a fast one." It is worth seeking the help of an expert if you are not comfortable in this area. Even honest mistakes will look bad.

How the budget actually looks can vary. Many funders require a specific format or give directions for the budget. If no direction is provided, the key is to ensure each section is clearly marked; that is, ensure your funder can determine at a glance how much of the funding will be earmarked for each major area of your project, but also be able to review a more detailed breakdown of the budget. Provide line items for each major cost and include summaries of each major area. For example, list the project salaries for each person involved and also include a summary total for personnel costs. Each summary total added together will equal the total amount of funds requested.

If matching funds are required, be sure to include the source and the amount in the budget. If this is missing, and it is a requirement, you will be disqualified. Because these funds are not included in the total amount you are requesting, make sure this is clearly indicated. Clarify the total amount you are requesting and the line items and summaries for each. Then clearly note the source of and amount of matching funds. These will all add up to create the project cost.

As the grant writer, you will be privileged to personnel salaries. This can be a touchy subject. When sending out the proposal for review to your committee and others willing to help, black-out the salary information. You can have another source review the accuracy of the budget information. Also be careful not to exaggerate salaries. You will be listing total salaries and the expected percentage of time each person will be spending on the project, thereby obtaining a salary range for the grant. While it can be tempting to inflate either the salary or expected time required for the project, avoid doing so at all cost.

Be sure to read the grantor's directions on allowable and non-allowable costs. Funders vary in what they will fund. If your budget includes items for costs that are not allowable by that funder, you give yourself immediate cause for rejection. Carefully read all information from the funder on how to create the budget and what you are required to include as well as what you are not allowed to include. If you are using a standard budget to work from, remember that each funder may have different requirements and rules, and you will need to take care to make the necessary changes to each proposal's budget.

Before submitting your grant, recheck all your numbers in the budget. It can be all too easy to accidentally type in an incorrect number or use an incorrect formula. If your numbers do not match, the funder will have every reason to wonder if you can successfully manage the money you are requesting. Check, check again, and check once more before submitting the proposal.

Please note: It is unethical to pay the grant writer using funds from the grant (i.e., paying the grant writer a percentage of the funds earned from the grant). If a grant writer is paid for his or her services, the funds to do so must come from another source outside of the grant funds. For example, you cannot pay a grant writer "10% of the funds earned from the grant."

Depending on the type of project you are creating, information on facilities and equipment may be included in the narrative or you may want to include additional information in an addendum.

Evaluation Checklist

Our Program

☐ Objectives can be measured quantitatively.

☐ Objectives can be measured qualitatively.

☐ Our target population is large enough to make measurable results meaningful.

☐ A quantitative outcome level has been established.

☐ A qualitative outcome level has been established.

☐ Objectives were met.

☐ Outcomes were documented.

Our Evaluation

☐ Evaluation criteria directly match objectives.

☐ Each objective has one evaluation criterion.

☐ Evaluation plans lists all strategies and procedures used to collect data.

☐ Data is presented in a clear format.

Some Evaluation Methods

✧ standardized test

✧ custom content-based assessment

✧ questionnaire (survey)

✧ inventory assessment

✧ student interview

✧ checklist (rubric)

Dissemination Ideas

The following are ways in which you might publicize your program (this includes advertising, educating the community, and disseminating the results). Your means of dissemination may be dictated by the desires of your funder and by your budget.

- ✧ educational conference (local, regional, or national)
- ✧ educational professional journal
- ✧ brochure
- ✧ school newsletter
- ✧ newspaper coverage
- ✧ radio interview or advertisement
- ✧ local television station segment
- ✧ Internet Web site
- ✧ educational magazine
- ✧ corporate marketing (including corporate logos)

Dissemination Tips

- ✧ be as specific as possible in your initial grant and stick to that plan
- ✧ identify the goals and needs of your funder and incorporate those into your plan
- ✧ always give credit to your funding source
- ✧ involve your funder whenever possible and if desired on their part
- ✧ involve students whenever possible
- ✧ involve parents/caregivers whenever possible
- ✧ utilize illustrations, photos, graphs, and samples of student work to make the presentation more interesting and "real"
- ✧ notify parents/caregivers of any and all publicity
- ✧ notify the school system's PR department of any and all publicity
- ✧ utilize technology whenever possible, including Web sites or presentation software
- ✧ choose one to two public faces for your program, and use those individuals for all publicity

Budget Checklist

Before you finish the budget, and in preparation to run the program, use the following checklist to make sure you have all bases covered. Some of the following will not be incorporated into the budget but may have school district costs associated with it.

Personnel

- ❑ teachers [total: _____ ; combined hours: _____]
- ❑ administrators [total: _____; combined hours: _____]
- ❑ aids [total: _____; combined hours: _____]
- ❑ parents [total: _____; combined hours: _____]
- ❑ evaluator [total: _____; combined hours: _____]

Equipment

- ❑ computers _____
- ❑ audio _____
- ❑ visual _____
- ❑ table and chairs/desks _____
- ❑ other _____
- ❑ other _____

Supplies

- ❑ office supplies _____
- ❑ food supplies _____
- ❑ other _____

Facilities

- ❑ location _____
- ❑ utilities _____
- ❑ janitorial services _____

Publicity

- ❑ print _____
- ❑ television _____

Budget Worksheet

	1	2	3	4	5
Personnel					
Equipment					
Supplies					
Services					
Evaluation					
Other					
Other					
Other					

0-7682-3078-0 *Grant Writing Made Easy*

Facilities and Equipment

Funders will want to know where the project will take place and any special equipment that is needed. If a program is going to take place on school property, for example, this can be addressed in the narrative, but may not require any additional information, particularly if facility needs do not need to be included in the budget. Similarly, if the program will make use of school equipment, a reference can be included but may not require special attention.

If, however, special facilities or equipment are needed, you may want to include additional information in an addendum. Does the project require a specific facility? Why is one facility preferred or required over another? Similarly, if special equipment is needed, you may need to provide additional information outside of what you cover in the narrative of the application. What to include for additional information is up to your best judgment. As with all aspects of your application, carefully review the funder's guidelines as to what is allowed for additional information, and then make the call if it is better to include information in the narrative or provide additional materials in an addendum.

Personnel

If allowed by the funder, include resumes or curriculum vitae for the primary personnel who will be involved in the project. If you know specific experts who will be involved, and you use their names in the grant, obtain their credentials and resumes to include in the addenda. Resumes can also be included for other key personnel who will be involved in the project, particularly those who have a history in or expertise in areas that will be fundamentally important to the project.

Ask for resumes as soon as you know who will be involved in the project. This will allow those involved time to update their information and get it to you. If possible, obtain them in electronic form so that you can reformat if desired in order to create unity in presentation (this does not mean the information will be changed).

Curriculum Vitae (CVs) can be included instead of a resume. Those in the teaching profession often use CVs instead of a traditional resume. The difference is that the CV includes a more involved professional history, including teaching credentials, courses taught, publications, and more. This can be useful when bringing in experts or when you need to highlight a person's credentials that are important to the grant but not necessarily highlighted to the extent needed for your purposes on their resume.

For help on writing a quality resume or CV, refer to the many books on the market that are written for this purpose. There are also a few organizations that certify resume writers if you would like to seek the help of a professional. This would likely only be necessary if your project is heavily dependent on the expertise or contribution of one or a few individuals.

Other Elements of a Grant

Cover Letter

The cover letter, or transmission letter, of your grant may seem like a minor detail that needs to be included before you put your proposal in the mail. But think for a moment about the purpose of the cover letter. Much like a cover letter to a potential employer when you are looking for a job, the cover letter to your proposal introduces your organization to a potential funder. It is the first thing the reader of your proposal sees. Why would you risk making a poor introduction?

Think of the cover letter as your first opportunity to sell your project. When writing an employment cover letter, the goal is to demonstrate what you have to offer a potential employer. The same is true for a grant cover letter. Your aim is to show a funder why you deserve to win the grant. State the purpose of your letter (your wonderful project), the amount you are seeking, and why your project meets the needs of the funder.

Remember, funders have their own agendas too. Your cover letter is the perfect opportunity to address the concerns of the funder. Although you will tailor your proposal to each grantor you apply to, your cover letter serves to immediately build a rapport with the grantor.

Just as you write other letters to a specific individual, do the same for your grant letter. If you already have an inside contact, use that person. Otherwise you may need to make a phone call or two to obtain the name of a person to whom you can address the letter. Always ask for correct spelling, even if the name is a common one. *Jane* may actually be *Jayne*; you just never know.

Consider waiting to write the cover letter until the proposal is finished. As with the abstract, you will be able to write a more compelling cover letter once you have completed all the steps of the proposal. Just as you want to do in a job search cover letter, you want to spark interest in your project with the letter. It is harder to "sell" the proposal if it has not been written yet. You will also be able to speak to the proposal with much more confidence and authority after it has been written because you will be intimately familiar with all aspects of the project.

Table of Contents

If your proposal ends up being longer (and meets the page requirements of the funder), you may want to consider including a table of contents (TOC). Even shorter proposals sometimes warrant the need for a TOC. If nothing else, it adds a sense of professionalism and courtesy to your application. If, however, the grantor is very specific about keeping the proposal short or only including specific information, forego the TOC. You never want to do anything that could hurt your chances; ignoring funders' directions is one way to do this!

Addenda

What you include as addenda will depend on the funder's requirements, the length of your proposal, and how much supportive material you need to include. Items that may be included as addenda include:

❖ Personnel information such as resumes and CVs, and any relevant information or work completed by key personnel such as publications and presentations

❖ Letters of support from parents, school officials, the community, and students

❖ Back-up material supporting the effectiveness of your project (particularly if you are basing your project on an existing one)

❖ Copies of your research or your research materials; this could include census data, school records, test scores, teacher qualifications, and any other material deemed important

❖ Information about your school or faculty (newspaper articles, copies of newsletters, and any other material that gives the funder information about your school and its mission). For example, is yours a large, inner city school or a small, multi-grade rural school? Are your students primarily minorities or from low-income families? Any pertinent information you can provide about who you are will help the funder get a sense for your school, your students, and your needs.

❖ Any legal documentation required by the funder

If you are not sure if a piece of information should be included, leave it out. Do not include fancy supplemental materials that you think may help your cause; they often will not. Videos, tapes, and CDs should not be included unless this type of material is specifically listed in the directions as being okay to send. Nor do you want to send every article or piece of publicity that has ever been written about your school. Only include those that support your project.

Sample Curriculum Vitae

Jessica Smith, Ph.D.
11 Educator Ln., Baltimore, MD 11111
Phone: 111-111-111   E-mail: jsmith@school.edu

1. Academic Degrees

PHD	Well-Known University	1998	Mathematics Education
MA	Well-Known University	1992	Mathematics Education
BA	Respected College	1985	Elementary Education

2. Relevant Professional Experience

2000–Present   Curriculum Director, Big School District, Big City, MD

Responsible for developing and overseeing curriculum in the areas of mathematics and science for grades K–12. Oversee textbook adoptions and monitor results of state standardized testing scores in mathematics and science. Conduct staff training for professional development.

1998–2000   District Math Coordinator, Medium School District, Well-Known City, PA

Responsible for implementing math curriculum, training teachers, and providing curriculum assistance to superintendent, principals, and teachers in a mid-size school district. Served on grant committee for grant projects "Mathematics in Motion," "Manipulatives Are Hands-On," and "Math and Science Are Related."

1995–1998   Principal, Elementary School, Little Town, MI

Managed day-to-day business of the school, oversaw discipline, managed staff of twelve teachers, aids, and assistants. Served on district textbook adoption committee for math. Implemented and oversaw mathematics technology initiative experiment at three district schools.

1985–1995   Teacher, Elementary School, Little Town, MI

Taught a variety of grades 2–4. Served on district's textbook adoption committee for math.

3. Presentations and Publications

Smith, J. (1999). "Making Your Mathematics After School Program Work."
A workshop presented at the annual National Council of Teacher of Mathematics (NCTM) conference.

Smith, J. (2001). "Professional Development Is Your Key to Good Teacher Relations."
A workshop presented at the annual Association for Supervision and Curriculum Development (ASCD) national conference.

Smith, J. (2001). "Evaluation and Assessment are Not Dirty Words." *Education Week*, Volume XXXX, Number 11.

Writing Checklist

Use this worksheet as both a checklist for your grant proposal and to brainstorm important points for each section.

❑ **The Abstract** _____

❑ **The Title** _____

❑ **Project Summary** _____

❑ **Statement of Need** _____

❑ **Goals and Objectives** _____

❑ **Project Methods** _____

    ❑ The Introduction: _____

    ❑ The Activities: _____

    ❑ Personnel: _____

❑ **Timetables** _____

❑ **Evaluation of Program** _____

❑ **Dissemination, Utilization, and Sustainability** _____

❑ **Budget** _____

❑ **Facilities and Equipment** _____

❑ **Personnel** _____

❑ **Other Elements of a Grant** _____

    ❑ Cover Letter_____

    ❑ Table of Contents _____

    ❑ Addendums_____

Addressing the Needs of Chosen Funders

After you have completed your research on funders, you should have a good idea of what each of your chosen funders are looking for. While the primary message will remain the same for each proposal you write, the format and emphasis will not. First and foremost, follow each funder's directions exactly. If you are unclear about anything in the directions, try calling the funder to obtain additional information. Most government grantors will be happy to speak with you; private funders will vary. It is beneficial to everyone for you to understand the directions, however, because it will save time for both you and the people reading your proposal.

Your targeted funders will be ones who have supported projects similar to yours, whether in subject matter, target audience (who is served by the project), size of grants, etc. Whichever element of your project is most closely related to the funder's history are those you will emphasize in your proposal. If possible, speak to these issues first, early in the narrative. Funders often support similar projects and organizations. Also remember that all funders have their own agenda. Government programs may need to find a program that fits with the guidelines predetermined for the funds available; show how your project meets those needs. Foundations may have a history of supporting female minorities; show how your program to increase science skills for girls will reach a broad audience of Hispanic and African-American students. Corporations support programs directly related to their marketing efforts; explain how your program designed to increase math scores among low-income students is the perfect match for that large manufacturer of calculators.

Proving the Need

More research? Yes! You may have noticed that grant writing has a lot to do with finding information. You need to demonstrate a need for the project in "hard facts" whenever possible. It may seem overwhelmingly obvious that a need for your project exists, but funders are not in your school on a daily basis, may not live in your community, and have only your word that there is a valid need. To convince funders that your project deserves funding, you need to show that the need exists in the first place.

How do you come up with the necessary proof? Thankfully, there are a variety of tools available, and the more you can use, the better. Just as funders will not take your word for the need, nor will they want to rely on only one source of evidence for the need. Also consider that when you conduct interviews or gather letters of support that each person may have a different viewpoint of the issue or may not understand what you need from them (many people have never written this type of letter, for example). Provide your "testimonial" sources with guidelines that will help them provide the necessary information but that will not sway their opinion in one way or another.

When using information in print, such as articles and other publications, remember to balance the findings with other sources of back-up information. Experts have their own

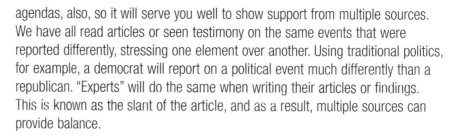

agendas, also, so it will serve you well to show support from multiple sources. We have all read articles or seen testimony on the same events that were reported differently, stressing one element over another. Using traditional politics, for example, a democrat will report on a political event much differently than a republican. "Experts" will do the same when writing their articles or findings. This is known as the slant of the article, and as a result, multiple sources can provide balance.

Once you have compiled your data, you need to do something with it. It is not enough to just send copies of everything with your proposal. As the grant writer, you need to analyze and explain the importance of the information for your readers. Why is it important that seventy-five percent of your students are from low-income families? What is the significance of the fact that the majority of your students failing reading are African-American boys? Tie-in the relevance of your findings to the need you are claiming and how your project will address the need.

Use charts, tables, graphs, and other illustrative means to show the results of your data and to present it in a meaningful way. These tools are easily understood by most people and can summarize the data in a way that writing about it cannot accomplish. This is obviously to your advantage, as you have limited space and need to convey a lot of information. It also provides visual breaks in the text and gives your proposal a nice appearance.

Possible Tools

Informational interviews: These can be conducted with a variety of people including teachers, parents, community members, educational experts, etc. The key when using interviews is to talk with a variety of people to present a range of opinions.

Group assessments and focus groups: What exactly is the problem? Different people will have different viewpoints. By working with a group, you can obtain information on how others view the problem and may learn some issues that you may not have thought of before.

Observations: Depending on your issue, conducting observations may provide valuable information. How are students interacting? How are families interacting? How are students behaving in class? People tend to look for things they want to see. Use a mix of observers when conducting this type of study to balance the results.

Surveys and questionnaires: As with interviews, when conducting surveys, aim for a mix in your respondents to give a better sense of the overall issue. Choose a lot of people to target as you have no idea how many you will hear back from. Also choose your questions carefully, and keep in mind that when you use open-ended questions, you will have a lot of responses to review, interpret, and compile into some form of report on results.

Public meetings: These can be very useful to help garner community support; however, they can also be difficult because you have to make people want to come, and you never know how many people will show up. Will the "right" people show up? If your project is targeting immigrants who are not native English speakers, will you be able to convince people in this group to come to a public meeting to speak on their own behalf?

Community profiles: Contact state agencies to obtain census and other community data. Check *www.[yourstate].gov* for links to census information in your state. Also look to the blue pages in the phone book to contact state, county, and city offices for population information. You may also find information in newspaper reports; police precinct reports; local health department reports; school report cards, test scores, and attendance figures; waiting lists for other community programs or organizations; and even anecdotal information from participants, staff, and community residents.

Articles, books, journal publications: When submitting articles and other related information, it should go unsaid that you want to choose a reliable publication. Well-known journals are a good choice. If your source is obscure, try to find the same information elsewhere. Also, when using this type of information, include data from other methods mentioned here so that you do not rely solely on one study, article, or expert's opinion for the reasons mentioned earlier.

Case studies: Case studies can be particularly helpful if they happen to come from a similar program or one after which you are modeling your project. If you are conducting your own case study, be sure to include enough detail to make it worthwhile. This method can take a lot of time. Use a small number of participants to ensure a comprehensive study. Be aware that bias can occur in case studies, so do your best to keep it neutral, and with observations, involve a mix of people to conduct the studies, review information, and keep it balanced.

Tests: This method can obviously be helpful for teaching or tutoring programs geared toward improving test scores or skills. By conducting "before" tests, you will have information for your proposal and also a starting point to use when tracking results throughout the program. Depending on the project, it may be necessary to develop a test. While this can be time intensive, the plus side to this is that you can use the test, or a version of it, in your program.

A Few Additional Notes
Census information can be useful but only if you put it into context. Merely showing that your target population exists does not prove a need; it only shows that the population lives in your area. Why is the target population in your area needier than the same target population in another area? Use additional information to demonstrate the need, such as income levels, employment, crime rates, and other data. Weave it together for the funder to show why your area is in greater need.

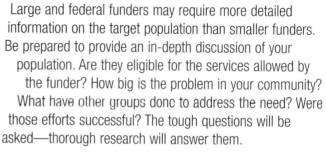

Large and federal funders may require more detailed information on the target population than smaller funders. Be prepared to provide an in-depth discussion of your population. Are they eligible for the services allowed by the funder? How big is the problem in your community? What have other groups done to address the need? Were those efforts successful? The tough questions will be asked—thorough research will answer them.

Where can you find this information? You can target your municipal, county, and state agencies that deal with your population. Examples of agencies include Public Health and Human Services, Housing Assistance, Labor and Industry, and Child Welfare Services. Find out if your city has a local census office.

Is there a university in your area? Take advantage of that library as well as your local library. Also consider calling around to various departments such as marketing and social services. There is a possibility that students have conducted the type of research that you are looking for. If not, you may be able to arrange a mutual working relationship in order to conduct the research you need.

As obvious as it sounds, contact the school district to find out what types of records they keep on file that may be of use to you. You may be surprised at how much information is at your fingertips. Use the scores on standardized tests to your advantage if appropriate, or show how the dropout rate in your school or district is higher than the national average. Compare your community's information to national averages to show that the need is in fact greater in your area.

Depending on the students you are targeting, police reports may provide the exact type of information you need. If your program is designed to reduce crime among youth, a report showing the problem will be required. Contact the local police to determine the policies on obtaining this type of information. You may be required to state why you need the information and how it will be used.

Writing Style

When in doubt, a formal writing tone is always better. Government proposals, in particular, require a formal tone. But this is not to say your tone should be too casual or friendly for private funders. The corporate world, for example, is steeped in business writing; your proposal should reflect that you understand this. Foundations, too, can be very business oriented, particularly large ones. Do not assume, for example, that because you are targeting a family foundation that an overly-friendly tone will be well received. When in doubt, opt for formal.

Even teachers can have moments of panic when it comes to writing, particularly when writing a document that is unfamiliar. It will not hurt to pick up a guidebook or two on business writing style. Strunk and White's classic, *The Elements of Style* (4th edition, Longman, 2000) is always a good choice. A number of sources are available for business style writing. If you are able to spend some money, there is always the comprehensive (and more expensive) *The Chicago Manual of Style* (15th edition, University of Chicago Press, 2003) or *The Gregg Reference Manual* (9th edition, Glencoe/McGraw-Hill, 2001). Check your libraries for these sources as well, but if you plan on doing a lot of grant writing, it can be worth it to purchase these tools.

Write using the active voice rather than passive whenever possible (there are times when passive is more appropriate, but in general, use active).

> *Active*   The school board voted on the measure.

> *Passive*   The measure was voted on by the school board.

Do not use contractions; they are too casual for business writing purposes. Also use the third person for the same reason. While addressing "you" is appropriate for this type of guide, it is not appropriate for a grant proposal. Third-person point of view emphasizes the subject and tends to use pronouns such as *he, she, it, we,* and *they,* as opposed to *you* or *I.*

What should you do if you are struck with a classic case of writer's block? Sometimes getting the first words down can be hard, and teachers may feel more pressure to write well the first go around (after all, if one teaches writing, one should be able to do it perfectly, right?). It can be difficult to turn off the inner censor and critic. Allow yourself to write the first draft however it comes out. Take advantage of some free writing exercises to get your thoughts flowing if necessary.

Doing all the research before you begin writing will also help because you will have a better idea in your mind of what you want to portray. By doing it piecemeal as you go along, you may find that your thoughts are not as well connected. Even though it will not come out perfect the first time, having a sense of the big picture can be helpful when you begin writing. Also remember to save the hardest parts for last. Do not write the abstract or cover letter until the end. If using an outline helps you organize your thoughts, write that first and use it as a guide. If you are the type who prefers a less structured approach, begin with the section that feels easiest. Whichever methods work for you, revising and editing will happen later, so how you get there in the first place is not as important as long as it works for you and gets you writing.

Keep your research organized. Find a method that works for you to keep track of all your research. This could be a notebook with dividers, an accordion file, or hanging files in a cabinet. When you begin writing the proposal, having easy access to your research will make the process easier as you need to reference material. (My method is to spread it all out on a big table as I write, but I do not necessarily recommend this method.)

Once you start writing, you will end up with material you are very happy with. It only makes sense to use this again in your other proposals. While there is no reason to make things harder on you, there are a couple of key points to remember. First, do not use the basic proposal "as is" for each funder. No matter how great the writing, you need to tailor it to each funder, even if that means changing some of your beautiful prose. The other extremely important thing to remember is to change references to the funder, remove names of people within the organization, and any other information that is directly written to a funder. If you are Ms. Jones and you receive a letter asking for a charitable donation but it is addressed to Ms. Smith, how likely are you to part with your money?

Legalese and "Grant Speak"

It can be very tempting to use fancy language to make your school and your grant appear "smarter." This practice can get you in trouble. For one, you never know who will be reading your application. Sticking to simple, straightforward language is your best bet. Funders may be turned off by attempts to impress them. Also, the meaning of your application may get lost in fancy language, thereby defeating your purpose.

While there are a few terms to understand regarding grant writing, such as being aware of the differences between goals, objectives, and methods, for the most part, grant writing is not much different from other business writing. Use clean, straightforward, and professional language in creating your grant. Refer to the "Overview of Grant Terms."

Other things to watch for are the use of clichés and buzzwords. Clichés are usually easy to catch if you are looking for them. Ask those who review the proposal to be on the lookout for overused phrases. Another danger is the use of buzzwords and jargon. As mentioned, the use of industry-specific jargon is discouraged because the person reading the proposal may not be familiar with the terms. There is no reason to confuse the reader if it can be simply avoided. Buzzwords are easy to use because they come to mind easily, but these words are overused and should be avoided. Phrases such as "user friendly" and even "at risk" do not mean much anymore. Clearly state the meaning rather than trying to rely on buzzwords to make the point. Even when writing concisely, use a few clear words to make a point rather than one buzzword.

When responding to an RFP, send your proposal ASAP or at least prior to the due date and determine the ETA so that it does not arrive JIT. Address it to a POC and consider including a SASP to confirm receipt. Explain the SOPs to be used for VA so the funder can determine the expected ROI.

Translation: When responding to a request for proposal, send your proposal as soon as possible or at least prior to the due date and determine the estimated time of arrival so that it does not arrive just in time. Address it to a point of contact and consider including a self addressed stamped postcard to confirm receipt. Explain the standard operating procedures to be used for value analysis so the funder can determine the expected return on investment.

Okay, the point is that acronyms can be annoying. In other words, UNA (use no acronyms), or at least keep them to a minimum.

While "political correctness" may be an overused phrase, in the case of writing for at-risk students, it is one to keep in mind. Because you will be writing about a broad range of people and ethnic groups, it is to your advantage to be aware of the most appropriate language to use. Also be wary of "talking down" about your targeted population; even if it is not conscious, this can occur when trying to emphasize the need.

In general:

 ✧ avoid contractions

 ✧ maintain consistency throughout in your headers, formatting, and punctuation

 ✧ avoid jargon

 ✧ use gender-neutral language

 ✧ write in the third person

 ✧ cut, cut, cut—keep your proposal brief and to the point

 ✧ write-out acronyms the first time you use them and avoid using too many

 ✧ avoid clichés

 ✧ keep key information in the narrative of the proposal; place supporting information in the addenda

 ✧ explain activities clearly

 ✧ use the active voice

Tips for Winning the Grant

Create a grant writing plan and checklist of every step and section of the proposal. Being organized will help keep your head clear and manage the process. Luckily, most teachers are natural organizers! Use your skills in this area to keep yourself and your team on track.

Always, always, always follow directions to a "t." Answer all the questions or address every issue the funder mentions. Some grantors are inundated with proposals and will look for any reason to discard an application. Competition for funds is just too strong. Make sure you get your proposal in on time, do not exceed page lengths, provide the budgetary information requested, and do not overlook required support. Not following directions is amateurish, and you cannot afford to take any risks. This is one of those areas where a mistake is inexcusable, because you were given the information up front.

Read the instructions. This is the same as the above, but it bears repeating.

Research, research, research. Grant writing is a lengthy, involved process and takes a lot of effort. Do not shoot yourself in the foot by writing a great proposal before researching funders. You will only do yourself a favor by taking the time to search out the most appropriate funders. This really cannot be stressed enough. Nothing will get your proposal thrown out quicker than submitting a proposal that does not fit the needs of the funder. Get a hold of the funder's 990 tax forms and find out what has been funded in the past and how much. Review the funder's guidelines to determine if there is an interest in your type of program. Are there restrictions? Do you know what they are?

Maintain continuity of information throughout the proposal. Just as you do not want a random expense turning up on the budget that has not been discussed elsewhere, you do not want random information popping up in one section of the narrative but not addressed anywhere else. Remember the relationship between the goals, objectives, and program methods? Refer back to these to help keep you on track.

As demonstrated in this book, sometimes key information needs to be repeated. This will naturally happen in your grant proposal as well. As you stress the pertinent issues about your project in the various sections of the proposal, some information will naturally come up repeatedly. While you want to avoid repeating the same information over and over, do repeat key elements strategically throughout in order to make your argument.

Write to your audience. If you have done your research, you will have an idea of the goals and mission of your targeted funder. While you do not want to change your project to meet the individual needs of each of your funders, you do want to stress the aspects of your project that are important to each. Say you are writing a proposal to implement a reading program geared toward Hispanic girls. Funder A has historically funded programs targeting minorities; for this funder, stress the impact that the program will have on the Hispanic population in your area. Funder B has historically funded programs geared towards girls; for this funder, stress that the program will have a lasting and positive impact on girls in your area.

Take hints from the funder's language. You can borrow key words from the funder's listings, for example, or from information on their Web site. What words do they use repeatedly? What is the tone? Incorporate these words in your proposal. Avoid using their usage word for word, but do take the language and reword it to fit your writing style. This can help create a familiar feel to your proposal, because you will be "speaking their language." Also consider using the funder's topics as headings in your proposal. This will make the correlation between information the funder requests and where it is located in your proposal.

Use tips from the funder to tailor your proposal. If the funder requires specific headings and sections, obviously follow them. But you can also take hints from information found about the funder and on their Web sites. Use similar language to theirs and stress points that the funder stresses. The funder will also realize that you carefully read the instructions and that you paid attention to detail, qualities that are desired in someone who will be directing a project.

In order to avoid mistakes, have multiple people familiar with the program review the proposal. This will ensure that all necessary elements are included for the project, and will give you a few extra "eyes" to review the proposal for simple mistakes such as following directions, grammar, punctuation, and typos. Be sure your reviewers have access to the funder's guidelines and instructions.

Send your proposal by regular mail well ahead of the deadline. Some funders, particularly public ones, will provide feedback or valuable information if there is enough time. For example, if your proposal is missing vital information, the funder may be willing to inform you of this. If your proposal is sent in too close to the deadline, you obviously will not have enough time to take advantage of this situation.

If you find yourself in a position where you have to submit your proposal using an expensive overnight carrier, you immediately demonstrate to the funder that you do not necessarily have good time management skills and that you are willing to spend money on expensive shipping options. (This holds true for electronic applications as well—if you want to take advantage of receiving feedback, you need to submit your application prior to the deadline.)

Before you send out the final proposal, review your checklist to ensure all items are included and in the proper order. Refer to the checklist provided earlier.

Then, proof, proof, and proof your proposal. Have others read it. Do not rely solely on your computer's spell check. Print out hard copies and read them word for word. Double check all items in the budget to ensure all calculations are correct.

Ask people who are not associated with the project to read key sections and tell you if it makes sense. Does the budget narrative fully explain the items listed in the budget? Does your abstract give an accurate portrayal of the project? Is your cover letter effective? These reviewers are as familiar with your project as your funders are. Their feedback can be invaluable.

Review the proposal again for any errors.

Reread the funder's instructions.

Review the proposal one more time.

Manipulative Math

Abstract

Recent research has shown that use of manipulatives in the mathematics classroom greatly enhances students' retention of mathematical concepts. Mathematical models and representations make abstract concepts concrete for students. The "Manipulative Math" program would train one hundred teachers in twenty K–5 elementary schools in the Medium City School District the best practices with reference to use of manipulatives in the math classroom. Teachers will attend a ten-day summer seminar held at the University of State run by that institution's professors of education in mathematics. Teachers will then utilize their new knowledge in their own classrooms and observe and assess their students' success. Teachers would meet two other times at three-month intervals—one for a refresher and one to report results. The program will be evaluated using rubrics, observation, student interviews, and a modified version of the math section of our state's standardized assessment. The requested funds would be used to purchase math manipulative kits, provide assessment materials, and to pay the fees for the University trainers and facilities.

Needs Statement

Medium City School District is in a medium-sized urban region. Seventy-six percent of our students receive free or reduced lunch and approximately one-third of our students are non-native English speakers. A recent survey of the results of our 4th grade math standardized test results found that only twenty-six percent of our students were proficient in math. The greatest area of difficulty was with problem solving and mathematical reasoning. Since implementing a computation-based textbook program three years ago, our students' math scores have dropped by 3.4 percent. This textbook programs focuses on written computation methods at the expense of more hands-on problem-solving methods. Compared to national test data, our students rank in the fifteenth percentile in math.

The importance of our program, "Manipulative Math," is supported by research by the University of State as reported in *Education Week* (see Addendum I), and by research from The Institute for Brain Research at the University of East Coast in the *Journal of Brain Science* (see Addendum II). Both groups have found that work with hands-on tools in the early (and later) years of mathematics study increases the retention of problem solving and mathematical reasoning. These skills lay the foundation for students to understand both basic computation and higher-level math concepts, such as statistics and calculus. This research also found that students who did not begin math study with a foundation in hands-on work fell farther behind their peers each year they attended school. By high school, students lagging behind had no hope of recovery. A hands-on intervention program that targets elementary-age students is the most effective course of action.

86 0-7682-3078-0 *Grant Writing Made Easy*

Goals and Objectives

The goal of "Manipulative Math" is to improve the problem solving and reasoning skills of K–5 students through work with hands-on math tools.

Objective I: Teachers will be fully trained to implement a hands-on math manipulative program in their classes.

Objective II: Students will demonstrate improved understanding of abstract math concepts through the use of concrete representations.

Objective III: Student state standardized test scores in math will improve by ten percent in one year.

Page 2

How Objectives Meet Standards

State math standards state that students will

 ✧ "Build new knowledge through problem solving";

 ✧ "Use hands-on tools to solve real-world math problems";

 ✧ "Apply a variety of strategies to solve problems"; and

 ✧ "Use representations to organize and record mathematical ideas and to model and interpret math phenomenon."

Page 3

Personnel

Program Director	Jose Incharge, Math Coordinator, Medium City School District
Program Assistant	Felicia Helpful
Teacher Trainers	Professors Mary Know, Ph.D., Gabriel Smart, Ph.D., and Simon Intelligente, Ph.D. of the department of education of University of State
Evaluator	Jerome Check, independent evaluator, formerly of XYZ Testing (a standardized test publisher)
Accountant	Susana Numbers, Assistant Superintendent of Finance, Medium City School District

Page 4

Budget

Personnel

Trainer	$XXX.XX
Trainer	$XXX.XX
Trainer	$XXX.XX
Evaluator	$XXX.XX
Personnel Total	*$X,XXX.XX*

Training Facility $XXX.XX

Training Materials

Lesson Plan Development	$XXX.XX
Manipulative Kits	$XXX.XX
Training Materials Total	*$X,XXX.XX*

Assessment $XXX.XX

Dissemination $XXX.XX

Grand Total   *$XXX,XXX.XX*

Page 5

Timeline

April	Finalize list of teachers involved in training.
May	Finalize curriculum and training schedule for teacher training.
June	Order manipulative kits and materials for training.
August	Teachers attend ten-day seminar at University of State.
September–November	Teachers utilize techniques in classrooms and monitor and record results; observation by teacher trainers.
December	Teachers attend 1-day refresher course.
December–February	Teachers utilize techniques in classrooms and monitor and record results; observation by teacher trainers.
March	Teachers attend 1-day refresher course.
March	Teachers conduct annual standardized testing and modified testing for program.
April–July	Standardized test results are evaluated; modified standardized tests scored and evaluated.
August	Results of program reported.

Page 6

Evaluation

Evaluation I: Teachers will be observed and assessed using a rubric based on material presented in ten-day seminar.

Evaluation II: Teachers will conduct individual interviews with students to assess understanding of concrete representations of abstract math concepts and will record qualitative results.

Evaluation III: Teachers will conduct testing using state standardized tests and a modified version of the math section of said test, and evaluate quantitative data.

Page 7

Dissemination

Tri-monthly reports on progress of the program will be made to the school board, the superintendent, and the funder. As well, informational pamphlets will be available in the school district main office, and a brief television feature (via our XYZ affiliate, WATV) will be used to inform the community of this valuable program. Results will be communicated in print form to the funder and in an online format on the school district Web site. Results will also be reported via the community newspaper, *The Medium City Times.*

Page 8

Follow-Up/Sustainability

Should this program be a success, additional funding would be required in the amount of $XX,XXX to purchase materials for the other elementary teachers in the district. These teachers would be trained by their peers in a seminar run and paid for by the school district. Annual testing and reporting would be made to ensure the success of the program.

Page 9

Addenda

Addendum I

    Article by the researchers at the University of State as reported in *Education Week*.

Addendum II

    Article by the researchers at The Institute for Brain Research at the University of East Coast in the *Journal of Brain Science*.

Addendum III

    Observation assessment form for evaluation of teaching practices to test effectiveness of trained teachers.

Addendum IV

    Sample interview form for assessment of student qualitative improvement.

Addendum V

    Sample modified state standardized math assessment used to evaluate quantitative results.

Addendum VI

    Curriculum Vitae for teacher trainers and evaluator.

Page 10

Chapter Four: Submitting the Grant

Ensure you maintain continuity throughout the document, both in terms of what is included and how it looks. You will be referring to similar bits of information throughout the proposal. Make sure that as you revise and make changes to the project that you revise and update the proposal if you have written parts of the document. Also take time to write each section (not the whole proposal) at the same time; at least the first draft of it. This helps keep your brain on track. Even the best "multi-taskers" can have difficulty returning to the middle of a section after taking a sizeable break from it.

So what does this thing look like? Visually, pretty much like any other document, with a few exceptions.

First, keep it easy on the eyes. Do you hate it when your students use huge fonts or change the margins on their papers in order to meet the required page length? Well, funders do not like too-small margins and tiny fonts. If you are limited in page length, work on the text, not the font size or margins. Use a font in an 11 or 12 point size and keep the margins reasonable; nothing less or more than an inch around all sides. It should go unsaid that if the funder lists specific font and margin requirements, they must be followed.

Keep the format the same throughout the document. Use similar headings for each section of the proposal, and take advantage of white space. Too much text can be hard to read. Use space between paragraphs if possible. Strategically place graphs, charts, lists, and tables throughout the document to break up the text. This can also serve to highlight important text by having it isolated.

Also take care not to overuse text effects. Too much use of bold, underline, italics, all caps, and other text alterations can make the document hard to read. Use these features sparingly to highlight only the most important points you want to emphasize. If too much is highlighted using special effects, your reader may be left wondering what is important—and wondering if *you* know what is important. You want the words to sell your proposal. If you have to rely on text effects to make the point, consider revising instead. These tips apply to your illustrative material instead. A fancy graph that does not convey meaningful information or is too difficult to decipher will defeat the purpose. And remember that all illustrative material must be included to support or clarify your narrative. Do not insert these items only for the purpose of breaking-up the narrative if they do not serve any other, more important purpose.

Keep the same font style throughout the document. Serif fonts (the ones with "tails" on the letters such as Times New Roman) are easier to read than sans serif fonts (such as Arial). Avoid mixing fonts within the same document except perhaps to highlight the title or other pertinent information. Begin each paragraph on a new line without indenting the first line. Also avoid using fully-justified text (where the text lines up on both the left and right sides of the page). The spacing between words becomes uneven and makes the text difficult to read. Draw attention to important information by using lists, tables, and charts. Use the header and footer functions to ensure that pages are numbered and in proper order.

Use quality paper but nothing too fancy. Standard weight copy paper is acceptable; too fancy of paper may give the impression that you are not cost conscious. Print the cover letter on your school's letterhead. Clip the pages of the proposal together rather than stapling and put the proposal in a full-sized envelope. There is no need for fancy binders.

Should you make use of fun graphics, color, and other options? This is also up for debate. Some grant writers suggest using these tools in moderation to help your proposal stand out. Others do not recommend it. Again, your choice will depend in part on the funder. Using a hot pink envelope for your application to the Department of Education is probably not a good idea.

Guidelines

Follow all funder guidelines regarding formatting, page length, and submission rules. Ignoring this information could immediately put your proposal out of the running. Also be sure to follow all guidelines and requirements regarding the order information is presented in and how the proposal should be delivered.

Multiple Submissions

How do you feel about all the junk mail that shows up in your mail box? Or spam in your email? For most people, this type of correspondence is unwelcome and quickly ends up in the recycle bin or the deleted mail folder. Advertisers who send out massive amounts of mailings do so in the hopes of hitting enough consumers to make it worth the effort. But when it comes to submitting proposals for funding, this is definitely not the approach to use, unless you want to waste a lot of time and postage.

It is acceptable and expected that you will target more than one funder. How many? Select only a few. And you will not send the same proposal to each. Every proposal you write needs to be tailored to the specific funder. Spamming proposals or sending the same query letter to a lot of funders will not yield good results.

So, you did the research and narrowed down your top choice of funders to four or five. Now what? Do you submit to one and wait to hear back before submitting to the next? Not necessarily. Your goal is to get funding, and your timeline may be somewhat limited, as you will most likely be conducting your project during the school year or over the course of a year.

Go ahead and apply to multiple funders. It is not uncommon, and chances are that you will not receive funding from every grantor you approach. Be aware that many funders want to be informed if you are making dual submissions. If you happen to receive funding from more than one funder, you have a few options. Can you expand the project? You may want to make the project bigger or ask a funder to support the project for an extended period of time. You might also work with a funder to see if they would be willing to support the continuation of the project following the original plan. If possible, work with the funder to see if they will support your efforts in some manner. What you need to do at this point is contact each funder, explain your situation, and provide suggestions for using the additional funds. Thank them for putting their faith in you and let them know how much funding you have received.

Be sure to use a reliable tracking system to manage your grants and applications, particularly when you are applying to more than one funder. The last thing you want to do is send the wrong correspondence to a funder. Keep all pertinent information for each funder in a file so that it is easily accessible to you. You will refer back to your files periodically, particularly when you receive funding or have questions for the funder during the process.

Electronic Submissions

More and more, funders are accepting applications online. Many consist of forms in which you will copy and paste information. Just as with other proposals, use online forms to tailor your application to the funder. Also follow the other writing "rules," write concisely (this may be even more important for online applications), and prepare your application well in advance. One of the dangers with online submissions is that it is very easy to hit that "submit" button before you are ready. Take time to read the application carefully, and print out the application and directions if possible; it can be difficult to read the information on the screen and it becomes too easy to miss important directions or key points.

Electronic grant applications may also be designed so that you can track and manage your program online. This allows for easy reporting to the funder and helps you keep organized. The U.S. Department of Education now offers an

e-grants system, as do most federal programs. To use the Education department's system, you will need to obtain a user ID and register with the department. See *http://e-grants.ed.gov* for more information. Electronic grants are likely the future of submitting and managing grants for all types of funders. While this will have a lasting impact on the grant writing process, the basics remain the same: proposals must be written to sell the project to the funder and answer all the basic questions that are required for paper applications. For more information on electronic grants, visit the Corporation for National and Community Service page on e-grants (*www.nationalservice.org*).

One danger with the electronic grant (and all proposals developed with the convenience of the computer) is the all-too-easy mistake of failing to change funder and recipient names when you use the copy and paste functions in the computer. Take extra care when using copy and paste functions. Also make note that if you upload complete documents, information such as who created the document and other privacy-related information can be accessed. If you use formulas or notes in a program, these can also be viewed by the recipient if you upload the page as is.

For more information on electronic grants, visit *www.cybergrants.com*.

Wait Time

Hearing back from funders can take weeks or months. This requires patience, but also careful planning on your part as it means you have to plan your project well in advance. Once you have sent in your proposal, it is okay to call about a week later (assuming you took the option of using regular mail as opposed to an overnight carrier) to verify it was received. You should be able to obtain this verification. At this point, inquire as to when you can expect a response. Although the guidelines may provide a general timeframe, it is a good idea to inquire during the phone call in the event anything changed between the times the guidelines were published and when you submitted your application.

Waiting to hear back from funders can be nerve-wracking and can also make it difficult to plan your upcoming year. Have a backup plan in the event you do not receive funding, whether this involves a different program or alternate funding. Whatever you do, avoid the temptation to call the funders or contact them regarding your application unless you have significant information that will add to your proposal.

How Are Proposals Evaluated?

What is important to funders? They want to know if your program will be successful, of course. Are the methods that you propose the best methods to reach the goals outlined in the proposal? Is the need obvious and well-supported? Are the objectives and activities clear? Does the organization seem to have a clear understanding of the problem? These and other questions will be used to evaluate the quality of your proposal.

Every section of your proposal is important. Everything included in your proposal should serve a purpose in demonstrating the quality and importance of your project.

Many funder guidelines include information on how the proposals are evaluated. Many, including government funders, use a point system. Each section of the proposal is worth a certain number of points, which lead to a total. The applicant with the best score gets the grant. For those who provide the point system, you automatically know going into it which sections will carry the most weight. While all sections are important (the smaller ones can lose you the grant just as easily as the larger ones can), pay attention to which areas carry more weight. This also gives you a clue as to what is most important to the funder.areas carry more weight. This also gives you a clue as to what is most important to the funder.

If You Are Rejected

Rejection is part of the process. Funders simply are not able to support all the projects they would like. As a result, competition is intense and funders have to turn down some proposals. Rejection is never easy, but it can be useful to your future funding efforts. Do call the funder to obtain feedback unless they specifically tell you not to call. Evaluators' feedback can be invaluable in determining what was wrong. Was it the project itself? Was the budgeting seen as too high or low? Was essential information missing? By obtaining this feedback you will know exactly what to work on next time. Otherwise you are left guessing, and this can be costly.

Ask the funder for the evaluator comments. Whether or not you will be able to obtain them will vary from funder to funder. When calling the funder, prepare yourself ahead of time with questions to ask regarding your proposal. First inquire if it is possible to obtain any feedback. If so, you will likely need to schedule a time to speak with the appropriate person. When you do speak to the appropriate person, be prepared with questions when you call, in the event you do not get a formal appointment.

When reviewing or listening to feedback, hold your comments. It is natural to feel defensive and want to make your case; however, by listening or reading carefully, you will find that you can obtain valuable information on why your grant was not funded. You may not agree with everything, but by keeping an open mind, you can come to a better understanding of why the funder made the decision. And this can help you when you write the next proposal.

Review all the comments you get from funders. Share them with your grant committee. How you respond to comments will be as varied as the different types of feedback you receive. Some funders may encourage you to revise and resubmit. Others may leave you wanting to ditch the program all together. Or you may decide that making a few minor alterations is the best approach. Whatever you decide to do after reviewing the feedback, remember that rejection is a part of the funding process. What one funder rejects may be the ideal project for another. Review your funder research to assure yourself that you are submitting to the best funding choices for your program and continue on the path that seems most appropriate. Thank your funders for taking the time to speak with you by sending a follow-up thank you letter. This is not only polite, but it reminds the funder of your professionalism, which they may remember next time you submit a proposal to them.

Take time to review your proposal. If it was one that you wrote at the last minute (as does happen to try to meet short deadlines), then you may have your answer there. Rework your proposal, taking the time it needs (and your students deserve). Have your reviewers go through the application and make copious notes (if your first proposal was done in a hurry, this step was likely missed). Carefully go through all the sections of the grant and review them for the necessary components.

Have you explained your project accurately? If the description, goals, objectives, and activities are not clear, you will not receive funding. Why would an organization support something they do not understand? Review the proposal from the point of view of someone who is completely unfamiliar with your project—even from the point of view of someone unfamiliar with the interior workings of the educational system. You never know who will read your proposal. Everything needs to be explained clearly.

Is the needs assessment convincing? If your research supporting the need for the program is not strong, the available funds may go to another proposal where the need is clearly stated and supported. It could be that you need to conduct more thorough or reliable research to support your claims and to paint an accurate picture of the needs of your target audience.

Did you carefully follow the funder's directions? This cannot be stressed enough. If instructions were not followed, money will not follow. Does your proposal fit within the funder's guidelines? If your project falls outside of what the funder supports, you will not receive the grant.

Are there any spelling, punctuation, or grammatical errors? Review the document for these mistakes. They give the impression of being unprofessional and sloppy.

Is all the supporting information, both within the narrative in the form of charts, graphs, and research, and in the addenda, easy to understand? Review all supporting data to see if there is anything that could be presented more clearly, included in a different order, or removed all together if it is not essential.

Are there any errors in the budget that were missed? Carefully review the budget for any errors, including typos, mistakes in calculation, listing items not addressed in the narrative, or anything that could be viewed as "padding" the budget. Ask a financial professional to review the budget if you created it yourself.

Proposal Tracker

Use the following worksheet to track your proposal after it has been submitted.

Name of Proposal		Date Submitted
Name of Organization	Contact Information	

Correspondence Log

Date/Time	Individual	Details

Rejected Proposal Assessment

Name of Proposal: _____

Submitted to: _____

Funder Comments: _____

_____

_____

Committee Review: _____

_____

_____

☐ abstract _____

☐ needs statement _____

☐ objectives _____

☐ standards _____

☐ personnel _____

☐ budget _____

☐ timeline_____

☐ addenda _____

☐ funder's directions _____

☐ spelling, punctuation, grammar _____

Next Steps: _____

_____

_____

_____

_____

_____

_____

_____

Future Plan

Future Proposals	Project Manager	Date Plan Completed	Date Proposal Ready for Submission

Grant Writer's Self-Assessment

The grant writing process for_____

❑   was an exciting and rewarding challenge._____

_____

❑   was an excellent collaboration opportunity for our staff. _____

_____

❑   was a positive professional development experience. _____

_____

❑   increased my interest in learning more about my field._____

_____

❑   was a great way to serve the school community. _____

_____

❑   was a way to develop and enhance relationships with administrators, principals,
    teachers, and educational professionals.

_____

❑   involved individuals from many areas of the school community. _____

_____

❑   improved the quality of my work in other aspects of my job/life. _____

_____

❑   was based on solid research and a definitive educational need._____

_____

Chapter Five: Managing the Grant

Congratulations! You have been funded. Now what?

First, celebrate.

Then, get to work.

When a grantor agrees to give you money for your project, you are entering into a contract with the funder. The funder agrees to give you money and you agree to perform the activities outlined in your proposal. How funders take care of the "fine print" will vary from one to the next. How much interaction you have with the funder will also vary. Some will request periodic updates and regular communication. Others will not want to hear from you again until you submit your final report of the project. Either way, you are developing a relationship with the funder, regardless of the amount of interaction.

The funder will likely reiterate the primary elements of the agreement—who the project will target and what it will accomplish. Work with your funder, verify their requirements at this point, and of course, thank them for supporting your work.

If the funder requests changes, work with them to reach a mutual agreement. You may not have any choice in the matter, such as when a funder agrees to give you money but not as much as you requested. Be prepared to be flexible with your program. If you are able to use the funding for a scaled-down project, go for it. As for other changes requested by the funder, work with your funder and maintain professionalism at all costs. Do not get defensive or try to argue your point to the extent that you risk losing the grant. If you feel strongly about a point, make your case and see what happens.

Begin making plans for your reports to the funder, whether those are periodic reports or only the final report. Track and record your progress throughout the program as you do the work. If you wait to compile your final report to the very end, you will create stress for yourself and leave open the possibility that you will miss key information. Keep a project file, notebook, or whatever organizational tool works best for you. Maintain detailed notes and create a draft of the final report as you go along. You will thank yourself later.

Budget Management

Obviously, maintaining the budget outlined in the proposal is ideal. But there may be circumstances where you need to make changes to the budget. Even if the bottom line does not change (if you want to "rearrange" the funds), you still need to contact the funder to explain the situation. You may also come to realize that you over- or under-budgeted the project. Again, immediate contact with the funder is the best option. Trying to hide the situation or make changes without notifying the funder can make you look unprofessional. It is much better to be upfront.

If you do not have much experience with the financial side of things, try to put someone on the team (ahead of time) who has experience in accounts management and can take care of this part of the process. If this is not possible, it is a good idea to have a couple of people track finances. This not only makes it easier to catch errors before they happen or soon afterward, but it also promotes accountability.

Tracking and Reporting Results

Some funders will want you to remain in contact and submit reports on a regular basis. Others will seem nonexistent until you submit the final report.

Carefully follow your objectives and activities throughout the program. These create the blueprint for your final report. Remember those evaluation methods (see pages 61–62) you described that you will use to demonstrate the success of your program? Now is the time to use them! Carefully document and maintain files on all aspects of the program. You will need these to create the final report, and you will need to provide your outside evaluators with all data from the program.

Determine from the funder how they want the final report submitted, and follow the directions. Work with the funder throughout the process, particularly if you find you need to make changes to the program for whatever reason (budget set too high or too low, expected resources not available, etc.).

Ensure you supply all required information to your evaluators. Their feedback is crucial to your final report.

Maintain professionalism throughout all aspects of applying for, running, and reporting on your grant. Each grant you successfully manage builds your reputation in the funding world. Take care to manage your project as outlined in your proposal, follow your budget and timelines, and submit all required reports and information. You will build a track record no matter how you run your project—for your reputation, your school's reputation, and your track record, it is in your best interest to manage the project as best you can. After you have developed a positive track record, you can refer to your history in subsequent proposals.

What Next?

After you have successfully managed a grant, then what? Hopefully it was a positive experience and served to help a number of students. Now is the time to build on your success and begin working on the next project. Grant writing is rarely something you will just do once. Also, by keeping involved in the process, you will be able to notice trends in funding and keep your name out there. Developing relationships with funders will also help you continue to obtain funds and serve your students.

If you opt to start small and work toward larger grants, each project you complete will build your reputation as a reputable grant manager. Each new project can take the successes of previous projects to build programs that are able to positively affect more students. As school officials and the community see the effects of a successful grant project, it will be much easier to gain support and letters of support for new projects. Encourage everyone involved in the grant process or affected by the process to make suggestions for new programs.

One of the biggest mistakes you can make is to stop seeking funds once you have run one successful program. Keep at it! By staying involved you become aware of grant funds and grant "speak," and you improve your grant writing abilities with each new proposal. Continue to seek other funds to continue not only what you have started, but to grow and expand new projects as well. Imagine the possibilities!

 0-7682-3078-0 *Grant Writing Made Easy*

Management Evaluation

Name of Project _____

Program Timeline _____

Program Manager _____

❑   The budget was met.

_____

❑   My program met a strategic need in my school community.

_____

_____

❑   Staff worked together well and maintained enthusiasm over time.

_____

❑   Students enjoyed the program.

_____

_____

❑   Parents were responsive to the program.

_____

❑   Quantitative data showed results.

_____

_____

❑   Qualitative data showed results.

_____

_____

❑   The funder was pleased with the results.

_____

_____

❑   Our next grant project will be…

_____

Chapter Six: Funders of Educational Grants

Nothing compares to a targeted research effort to find funders that will support your specific project. Research is crucial to your grant seeking success; it is perhaps the most important thing you will do in your quest for grant funds. The following is a sampling of funders that support education activities; many funders are partial to projects that address populations needing intervention for a variety of reasons (remember to specifically define your target audience) and those that address NCLB issues.

Note: Most of these Web sites reference home pages of the following organizations. To find the specific documents mentioned, please navigate the Web site. Most of these will be easy to find. We have not included specific Web page addresses because many of these URLs change from month to month and are not reliable.

Federal

U.S. Department of Education
"Guide to Education Programs"
http://www.ed.gov

U.S. Department of Health and Human Services
http://www.hhs.gov (Find the "Grants and Funding" page.)

The Catalog of Federal and Domestic Funding
http://www.cfda.gov

Foundations

The Annenberg Foundation
http://www.whannenberg.org
Headquarters Office
Radnor Financial Center
Suite A-200
150 N. Radnor-Chester Rd.
Radnor, PA 19087
(610) 341-9066

The Arthur Vining Davis Foundation
http://jvm.com/davis
Dr. Jonathan T. Howe
Executive Director
225 Water Street, Suite 1510
Jacksonville, FL 32202-5185
(904) 359-0670

ASM International
http://www.asminternational.org

Bamford-Lahey Children's Foundation
Funds projects related to developmental language disorders
http://www.Bamford-Lahey.org
2995 Woodside Road, Suite 400
Woodside, California 94062

Beaumont Foundation of America
http://www.bmtfoundation.com
P.O. Box 1855
Beaumont, TX 77701
1-866-546-2667

Carnegie Corporation of New York
http://www.carnegie.org
437 Madison Ave.
New York, NY 10022
212-371-3200

The Dana Foundation
http://www.dana.org
745 Fifth Avenue, Suite 900,
New York, NY 10151

The Educational Foundation of America
http://www.efaw.org
35 Church Lane
Westport, CT 06880-3515
203-226-6498

Ezra Jack Keats Foundation and Programs
http://www.ezra-jack-keats.org
Ezra Jack Keats Minigrants
450-14 Street
Brooklyn, NY 11215-5702

The Edward E. Ford Foundation
http://www.eeford.org
Robert W. Hallett, Executive Director
The Exchange
1122 Kenilworth Drive, Suite 105
Towson, MD 21204
410-823-2201

Ford Foundation
http://www.fordfound.org
320 E. 43rd St.
New York, NY 10017
212-573-5000

Bill and Melinda Gates Foundation
http://www.gatesfoundation.org
PO Box 23350
Seattle, WA 98102
206-709-3100

National Foundation for the Improvement of Education (NFIE)
NFIE, sponsored by the National Education Association, provides grants for
teachers, educational and professional resources, and publications.
http://www.nfie.org
1201 16th Street, NW Washington, DC 20036
202.822.7840

National Science Foundation
http://www.nsf.gov
4201 Wilson Boulevard
Arlington, Virginia 22230, USA
703-292-5111

Tiger Woods Foundation
http://www.twfound.org
7506 Slate Ridge Blvd.
Reynoldsburg, Ohio 43068
614-856-9460

The Wallace Foundation
http://www.wallacefunds.org
2 Park Ave., 23rd Floor
New York, NY 10016
212-251-9700

Corporate

The Allstate Foundation
http://www.allstate.com/foundation
2775 Sanders Rd. Suite F3
Northbrook, IL 60062-6127
847-402-5502

The Coca Cola Foundation
http://www2.coca-cola.com (Look in the "Citizenship" section.)

GE Fund
http://www.ge.com (Find the "GE in the Community" page.)

Hitachi Foundation
http://www.hitachifoundation.org
1509 22nd Street, NW
Washington, DC 20037-1073
202-457-0588

Home Depot
http://homedepotfoundation.org

IBM Foundation
http://www.ibm.com (Find the "Community Relations" page under "About IBM.")
IBM Corporation
1133 Westchester Avenue
White Plains, New York 10604

Lucent Technologies
http://www.lucent.com (Find the "Philanthropy" page located in the company information section.)
600 Mountain Avenue
Room 3C-209
Murray Hill, NJ 07974
908-582-7909

Nike
http://nikebiz.com

Sprint Foundation
http://www.sprint.com (Locate information about sponsorships and funding in the corporate information section.)

Texas Instruments Foundation
http://www.ti.com/corp/docs/company/citizen/giving/index.shtml

Toshiba America Foundation
http://www.toshiba.com (Information about this foundation is located on the "About Toshiba" page.)
1251 Avenue of the Americas
41st Floor
New York, NY 10020
212-596-0620

Toyota
http://www.toyota.com (Go to the "Community Care" page under "About Toyota.")

W.K. Kellogg Foundation
http://www.wkkf.org
One Michigan Avenue East
Battle Creek, MI 49017

Finding Local Grant Money Resources

How do you locate local money? In part this depends on where you live. In the case of corporate giving, for example, your best bet in obtaining funds is if there is a corporate presence in your area. Companies like to give to the communities where they do business because it is good for public relations and also important for employee morale. Employees often have input about the types of charity work that should be supported. Education is often one of the top priorities in corporate giving, so contact the local offices of businesses in your area to learn more about the company's giving policy. Also remember that many companies prefer to give in-kind gifts (such as equipment) rather than funding an actual grant.

To learn about potential city and statewide funding, try calling the agency's local numbers to inquire about funding opportunities. Refer to *www.statelocalgov.net* for information on statewide agencies. Also try *www.[yourstate].gov*, for your state's government Web site, and then use the search tool to search for grants. Because your search will likely return thousands of hits, you may also want to try entering a more narrowed search such as "education grants." Use both broad and narrow searches to obtain a variety of hits. One search may return results that another misses. Also visit the agency's Web sites for information on potential funding opportunities.

Visit the library! Again, do not overlook the potential goldmine that can be found at the local library. The reference librarian may be able to direct you to local resources or may even know of local funding opportunities. Also visit the library's Web site and check for links to funders.

Use your networking contacts. Keep in touch with your school's administration, other teachers, and business and community networks. Put the word out that you are seeking funding. Also share what you find with other teachers and schools seeking funding. You may hear of another school seeking monies for a different project; if you come across a good funding opportunity, share the news. The favor is likely to be returned.

Attend local and state conferences, workshops, and training opportunities related to grant writing and professional development. Take advantage of any grant writing opportunities available, from free training programs hosted by the library or school system community education to formal training workshops.

Put your school on newsletter lists. Get on the mailing lists for agency information and RFP notifications. Not all will be the match you are looking for, but the information will help you stay abreast of local funding trends, which can help you determine the appropriate direction for your program and help you prioritize from among a number of program ideas. Also get familiar with local and state representatives and obtain an idea of the types of programs they support. If possible, meet with them at various functions. Take a few minutes to talk with them about their priorities and how those fit with your school's mission and priorities. If there is an interest in your project, these people may prove to be key contacts or be able to provide you with references or recommendations on who to contact. Congressional representatives also have government grant resources available through their offices. If your library has limited federal information, it may be worth a trip to the state capital to do a little research. And do not forget about your state's governor's office. This office has access to a wealth of state information.

 0-7682-3078-0 *Grant Writing Made Easy*

Free and Inexpensive Materials

If you find that you do not need a grant or that you need to supplement your program with items not funded by your grant, look for free or very inexpensive materials or curricula that you can use. The following list contains some sources.

The Aluminum Association, Inc.
http://www.aluminum.org

For teacher materials, go to the recycling section of the Web site. The Aluminum Association has a partnership with Habitat for Humanity called "Can's for Habitat." Information on how to get involved can also be found at *http://www.cansforhabitat.org*.

Bureau of Public Debt
U.S. Department of the Treasury
http://www.publicdebt.treas.gov

On the Web site, go to the savings bond section and find the teacher materials. There is free information about savings bonds in a student-friendly format as well as access to a savings bond calculator that is a great tool for teaching about the value of bonds over time.

National Council of Teachers of Mathematics (NCTM)
Headquarters
1906 Association Drive, Reston, VA 20191-1502
703-620-9840
fax: 703-476-2970
http://www.nctm.org

On the Web site, find the "Illuminations" section, which provides free sample math lesson plans and Web resources, sometimes interactive tools, based on the NCTM standards.

National Gallery of Art
http://www.nga.gov

Offers teacher's kits covering specific artists, time periods, or art styles. Kits include booklets, slides, and study prints. Go to the "Education Resources" section of the Web site. Kits are free on loan.

Free-Loan Teaching Resources
email: EdResources@nga.gov
Teacher Resources
phone: (202) 842-6263

National Oceanic and Atmospheric Administration
National Weather Service
1325 East West Highway
Silver Spring, MD 20910
http://www.nws.noaa.gov

This online information service offers weather-related data, maps, and documents.

The President's Challenge Physical Activity and Fitness Awards Program
http://www.presidentschallenge.org

The President's Challenge Physical Fitness awards program. This program encourages students to become more physically fit through exercise and participation in sports. Offers free online tools to track student records. You can also order awards, apparel, and teaching aids for a minimal fee.

Smithsonian Office of Education
http://www.smithsonianeducation.org/educators

Offers resources on a variety of subjects, including art & design, science & technology, history & culture, and language arts.

State and Provincial Information

Tourism offices are happy to provide teachers with informational packets on their states or provinces. Write to your state tourism board, or find the Web site. One example of a state Web site is *http://www.state.mi.us*. This is for Michigan; simply fill in your state's postal code in place of the "mi." To find a Web site for a Canadian province, try the following, and fill in your province's postal code: *http://www.gov.bc.ca* (bc = British Columbia).

U.S. Fish and Wildlife Service
http://www.fws.gov

Go to the kids and educators link. Offers curriculum resources on a variety of animals, habitats, and endangered species. Free. Also can order audio-visual materials for a fee.

Drug Enforcement Administration
http://www.dea.gov

Offers "Get It Straight," a free online drugs fact book written by teens.

Energy Efficiency and Renewable Energy Clearinghouse
http://www.eere.energy.gov

Offers teacher resource packets for elementary, middle, and high school grades that includes activities to promote energy conservation. If interested in other sources of information on energy, request the publication titled *Energy Education Resources: Kindergarten Through 12th Grade* or use the online service for information on renewable energy technologies. Free.

Overview of Grant Terms

501 (c) (3): tax code that defines nonprofit, tax-exempt, charitable organizations (required for applying for grant funds)

abstract: brief overview of the entire project

activities: the methods used to meet objectives

addendum: additional information attached to the proposal narrative or budget to provide additional information about the proposal

allowable costs: costs that the funder agrees to cover

authorized signature: signature of the individual who is legally responsible for your school or institution (this may be the principal or a superintendent)

award: a gift of grant money

block grants: funds distributed by the federal government to cities or states to be distributed based on population

budget: fiscal plan of organization and project plan; details how grant monies will be spent

community foundation: a nonprofit organization that makes grants on behalf of multiple organizations within a community

competitive grant: grant awarded through competitive application process

curriculum vitae (CU): an account of one's carreer and qualifications (usually more detailed than a resumé)

demographics: description of a population in a given area

direct cost: amount necessary to fund a project, not including indirect costs

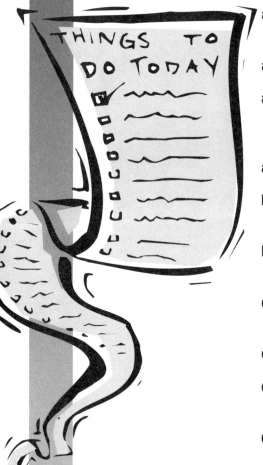

0-7682-3078-0 *Grant Writing Made Easy*

discretionary grants (foundation): grants allowing trustees to support charities that they care about but are outside of the organization's guidelines

discretionary grants (government): those available from a higher level of government at its discretion and depending on available funds, through a competitive process

dissemination: section of the grant that describes how the results from the grant will be shared with others

eligibility: criteria to determine who can submit an initial proposal

evaluation: how the project will be reviewed for reaching measurable changes as a result of the funded project

formula grants: publicly funded grants that reimburse your school for services already performed

foundation: private organization usually devoted to a cause or issue that may award fund to further that cause.

goals: broad statements describing what the project hopes to accomplish

grantee: organization or individual who receives the award

grantor: organization or individual who gives the award

indirect cost rate: a formula used to calculate indirect costs

indirect cost: a portion of the grant or contract that may be used for costs not directly related to the program (usually a percentage of the total grant)

in-kind gifts: receiving free goods or services instead of grant funds

letter of support: letter written by someone involved with or affected by the project, such as school administrators, teachers, parents, and community members; written to the funder in support of the project; typically included in the addenda of the proposal

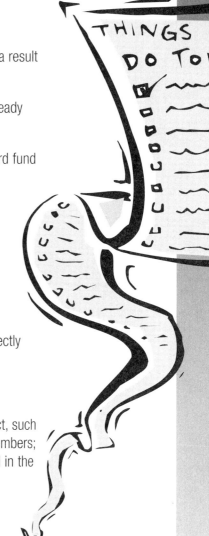

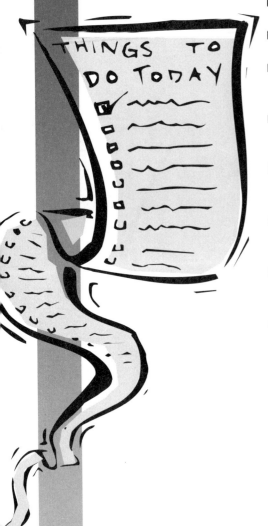

matching funds: a percentage of funds that the requester of the grant must provide before the funder will fund the project

metrics: business term referring to measurable outcomes of a project

mini-grants: small grants typically under $5,000

need-based grants: grants awarded based on the need of the applicant as the primary criteria

needs assessment: statement and proof of need for the project; details who will be served by the project and why the need exists

No Child Left Behind (NCLB): federal act to ensure quality improvement in education

objectives: measurable activities for reaching the goals of the program; usually listed directly under the goal the objective supports

organizational budget: budget that includes all operating expenses plus expenses for each program

outcomes: measurable results of a project

private grantors: grants funded by private entities including individuals, foundations, charities, trusts, or corporations

processes: how the program will be carried out

project grants: public grants that are competitive

public grantors: grants funded by the states or federal government

qualitative data: data that is observed and gives a general picture of quality

quantitative data: data that can be counted, recorded, and represented by numbers

query letter: letter to funder inquiring about the funder's guidelines and providing a synopsis of the project; asks the funder about the interest in seeing a full proposal

stakeholders: individuals or groups affected by the grant, including the target population and those connected with the target population

sustainability: how the project will continue after the grant has officially ended

target population: the group of people directly affected by the grant

Additional Online and Print Resources

Note: Most of these Web sites reference home pages of the following organizations. To find the specific documents mentioned, please navigate the Web site. Most of these will be easy to find. We have not included specific Web page addresses because many of these URLs change from month to month and are not reliable.

Federal

(Check your local library for these resources as many are quite expensive.)

Catalog of Federal Domestic Assistance (CFDA)
Superintendent of Documents
PO Box 271954
Pittsburgh, PA 15250-7954
866-512-1800 or 202-512-1800
http://www.cfda.gov

"Federal Register"
(5x/week publication supplementing CFDA)
Superintendent of Documents
PO Box 271954
Pittsburgh, PA 15250-7954
866-512-1800 or 202-512-1800
http://www.archives.gov

"National Science Foundation Bulletin"
http://www.nsf.gov

"NIH Guide for Grants and Contracts"
http://www.nih.go

United States Government Manual
Lists personnel, addresses, and telephone numbers for all agencies and departments
Superintendent of Documents
PO Box 371954
Pittsburgh, PA 15250-7954
http://bookstore.gpo.gov

"Education Grants Alert"
Weekly publication covering federal and private funding
Federal Grants and Contracts Weekly
Weekly information on RFPs
Aspen Publishers, Inc.
http://www.aspenpublisher.com

Federal Directory
Carroll Publishing
http://www.carrollpub.com

 0-7682-3078-0 *Grant Writing Made Easy*

Federal Yellow Book (subscription publication)
Includes directory of federal departments
Leadership Directories, Inc.
http://www.leadershipdirectories.com

GovSpot
http://www.govspot.com

U.S. Department of Education
http://www.ed.gov

No Child Left Behind
(legislation information)
http://www.ed.gov/nclb

Agency for Healthcare Reasearch and Quality
http://www.ahcpr.gov

National Institute for Literacy
http://www.nifl.gov

National Center for Education Statistics
http://www.nces.ed.gov

United States House of Representatives Committee on Education and the
Workforce
http://edworkforce.house.gov

Foundations

The Foundation Center
(Review as many publications from the Foundation Center as possible as all are
excellent resources; visit your local library.)
79 Fifth Avenue, Dept ST
New York, NY 10003-3076
800-424-9836
http://www.fdncenter.org

The Council on Foundations
http://www.cof.org

Philanthropy News Network Online
http://www.pnnonline.org

Corporate

(Check your local library for these sources as many are expensive.)
Corporate Giving Directory, 26th edition
by Deborah J. Baker (Taft Group, 2003)

The National Directory of Corporate Giving, 8th edition
by David L. Clark (The Foundation Center, 2002)
http://www.fdncenter.org

Million Dollar Directory: Top 50,000 Companies
(Dun & Bradstreet, 2003)
http://www.dnb.com

Standard & Poor's Register of Corporations, Directors and Executives: 2004
(Standard & Poor's Corporation, 2004)
http://www.standardandpoors.com

*Funding Sources for Community and Economic Development 2004/2005: A Guide to
Current Sources for Local Programs and Projects*
(Oryx Press, 2004)

Funding Sources for K–12 Education 2004
(Oryx Press, 2004)

Wealth ID
(strategic fundraising solutions)
http://www.wealthid.com

Hoovers Online
(business information resource)
http://www.hoovers.com

Business Journal's Book of Lists
http://www.bizjournals.com

Securities and Exchange Commission (SEC)
http://www.sec.gov

General Online

Gifts in Kind
http://www.giftsinkind.org

Grantmakers Concerned with Immigrants and Refugees
http://www.gcir.org

The Grantsmanship Center
(Offers training and a wide range of information.)
http://www.tgci.com

Trends in International Math and Science
http://www.nces.ed.gov/timss

Unsung Heroes Award
http://www.unsungheroes.com

National Staff Development Council (NSDC)
http://www.nsdc.org

SchoolGrants webpage
Iittp://www.schoolgrants.org

Education World
http://www.educationworld.com

eSchool News Online
http://www.eschoolnews.com

Library Spot
http://www.libraryspot.com

Non-Profit Guides
http://www.npguides.org

Fundsnet
http://www.fundsnetservices.com

General Print

Creating Foundations for American Schools
by David G. Bauer (Jossey-Bass, 2000)

Get That Grant: Grantwriting from Conception to Completion
by Barbara C. Bader and Steven Carr (Community Systems, Bozeman, Montana)

Grant Writing for Dummies
by Beverly A. Browning (Wiley Publishing, Inc., 2001)

Grants Management: Planning, Implementing, Monitoring, and Evaluating Grant-Funded Programs
by Barbara C. Bader and Steven Carr (Community Systems, Bozeman, Montana)

The "How To" Grants Manual: Successful Grantseeking Techniques for Obtaining Public and Private Grants, 5th edition
by David G. Bauer (Praeger Publishers, 2003)

The Only Grant Writing Book You'll Ever Need: Top Grant Writers and Grant Givers Share Their Secrets!
by Ellen Karsh and Arlen Sue Fox (Carroll & Graf Publishers, 2003)

The Principal's Guide to Winning Grants
by David G. Bauer (Jossey-Bass, 1998)

Successful Grantseeking: A Comprehensive Guide to Developing Proposals, Finding Funders, and Managing the Grant Process
by Barbara Bader, Ph.D. and Steven Carr, M.S.W.
(Community Systems, PO Box 516, Bozeman, MT, 59771-0526, 406-587-8970)

The Teacher's Guide to Winning Grants
by David G. Bauer (Jossey-Bass, 1998)

Technology Funding for Schools
by David G. Bauer (Jossey-Bass, 2000)

Notes